D1521413

College After 30

A Handbook for Adult Students

Caryl Chudwin and Rita Durrant

Contemporary Books, Inc.
Chicago

Library of Congress Cataloging in Publication Data

Chudwin, Caryl.
   College after 30.

   Bibliography: p.
   Includes index.
   1. Continuing Education.   2. College student orienta-
tion.   I. Durrant, Rita.   II. Title.
LC5219.C52   1981   374   81-65193
ISBN 0-8092-5933-8   AACR2
ISBN 0-8092-5931-1 (pbk.)

Published by Contemporary Books, Inc.
180 North Michigan Avenue, Chicago, Illinois 60601
Manufactured in the United States of America
Library of Congress Catalog Card Number: 81-65193
International Standard Book Number: 0-8092-5933-8 (cloth)
                                    0-8092-5931-1 (paper)

Published simultaneously in Canada by
Beaverbooks, Ltd.
150 Lesmill Road
Don Mills, Ontario M3B 2T5
Canada

To John Durrant and Manny Chudwin
in love, friendship, and admiration

Contents

PART IV: FACING PROBLEMS

PART V: STUDY SKILLS—HOW TO STUDY AND GET GOOD GRADES

Introduction

Hindsight is always easy. "If only I knew then what I know now" is a familiar refrain in all of life's experiences—from rising to the top of a corporation to rearing children.

When we returned to college in the '70s as reentry students, we entered with the innocence and trepidation of lambs going to the slaughter pen. Advice for returning students was scarce, if not altogether unavailable, and was written either in thesis jargon or in boringly simplistic terms. What we needed to know were some good coping mechanisms for home and school. Could we really be friends with a husband who wanted to go to the movies when we wanted to stay home and read? Who could help us best to cut red tape in the bureaucracy of academe? If we flunked a course, were we doomed to failure? What was the best way to prepare for an exam, to write a paper, to plan for our future?

Our reentry into college was indeed a fantastic experience in a community of scholarship where learning became the "real world." Yet, in reviewing those recent years, we realize that our college years would have been even more enjoyable and educationally profitable if we had been offered some straight-from-the-shoulder information and tips in advance. Had we approached it as better educational consumers, we would have saved both time and money.

To these ends we dedicate our book, *College After 30: A Handbook for Adult Students,* whose contents reflect not only our own experiences, but those of other students, professors, administrators, and counselors, who have generously filled in our questionnaires and participated in our interviews.

PART I:
GEARING UP FOR COLLEGE

1

A Profile of the Returning Student

If you are over twenty-five or thirty and under one hundred years old, starting your college career from scratch or with prior credits in your hip pocket, you fit the profile of the reentry student. One-third of all college students now fall into the mature adult category.

Like the army recruiter in the poster of Uncle Sam pointing his finger and indicating, "We Want You," college administrators all over the country are beckoning reentry students. With the drop in the college-age population, returning students have become the hottest item on the student recruitment scene. Their numbers represent the 2–4 percent annual growth in college enrollment during the 1970s. Further projections of 25 million adults in organized educational activities in 1990 means that you can pick and choose from a growing number of continuing education programs best suited to your needs.

Walk into a class today and view the adult learners. You will find housewives seeking new identities and engineers and business executives updating skills. Working people, both skilled and unskilled, who had never considered

1

higher education before, have joined the ranks of returning students.

A man who returned to college in his forties describes his experience:

> I worked as a punch press operator in a factory located near a community college and passed its campus every day. The students looked so happy and energetic. I said to myself, "I wonder if I could do it, if I'm smart enough." Never having gone to college, my doubts were deep. Twice I drove into the school parking lot and twice I didn't get out of my car. The third time I said, "Oh, hell. Why not?" The steps from my car to the admissions office were the longest steps I've ever taken. They led me to a new career and the personal esteem I had never before experienced.

Many others who have dropped out or flunked out are coming back to school, this time with a new sense of urgency and determination.

Helen V. dropped out of high school when she was seventeen because she was bored. Later she completed high school and attended a community college where she did poorly in her schoolwork. Opting for the working world, she left school again. In the next few years she worked her way up to a level of some responsibility in a large firm. Yet she felt something was missing.

"I had lots of good ideas at work," she said, "but no theories to back them up. The college graduates seemed to be getting attention and the good promotions. I was really disgusted with myself. These people were no smarter than I. My only alternative was going back to college.

"When I made an appointment with the counselor, she pulled out my dismal record and noted that I had done poorly. 'Why,' she asked, 'if you did poorly before, do you think you are going to do any better this time?' I didn't hesitate to answer. I told her, 'This time I want it.'"

All racial and ethnic groups have also joined the march

back to school. Schools in major cities are traditionally the place where waves of "new" students enroll seeking education to better themselves. Europeans, blacks, Hispanics, Appalachians, Vietnamese, Iranians are all coming in their own time. Hispanics alone increased their enrollment by 13 percent in a recent two-year period.

For other reentry students, college represents a need to know in a world that has become increasingly complex and computerized. "I was getting stale," says one woman who found herself growing apart from her family for lack of common interests. In this case, it was her husband who insisted she become a student.

> It was meant to be a silver anniversary gift. My husband drove me to the nearest community college and insisted that I sign up. I remember plowing through snow drifts in the bitter cold on a February morning to find our way to the portable admissions office. I sat waiting to talk to a counselor in my Butte knit, a puffed up plastic hairdo, and funny-looking horn-rimmed glasses trimmed with rhinestones. I looked like I belonged in the supermarket, not a college admission office. Deep down I felt excited and frightened. It took a while for the anxiety and out-of-place feeling to leave me, but the excitement stayed and stayed.

Many other students who *have* attended college before are returning to upgrade information in their fields in order to avoid obsolescence. Still others are enrolling in graduate school to earn additional or advanced degrees. In a report of nearly 2,000 adult students sponsored by a College Board study, 83 percent named some transition in their lives as the motivating factor for going back to school. An engineer, who worked in a steel mill for twenty years and went back to the university to earn a Master's degree in Business Administration, reports, "Although my degree in Engineering has made it possible for me to earn a good living all these years, my division could be phased out. I wasn't too worried about financing my education. As a veteran, I was able to get a state scholarship even though my GI benefits had run out. I would like to take an early retirement. Someday I'll have a second career. Maybe even a third!"

Carla's problem was different. She frankly called herself a "worrier."

> When Jim and I were married, I quit school and went to work. We always wanted to have two children and, when our last daughter was born, I felt that all my dreams had come true. Then Jim became ill and I realized I would have to help with the family income. I am now completing work on a nursing degree. My husband is working again and makes a really decent salary, but I think most families will need to have two incomes in the future. These are very hard times for young families, and it doesn't look as if the future will be much brighter.

Thousands of students who are back in school for a second time do so with a greater feeling of determination. Men and women who dropped out of college to go into the service, get jobs, get married, support a family, or just to "hit the road" have returned to the American college campus. Americans still believe that a college degree is a key to a successful and happy life.

As you can see, there is really no such person as a typical adult student. Each student shares only one thing in common with all others—a return to study after a period of time devoted to other endeavors.

2

Planning for Reentry

Whatever your impetus for considering going to school, we urge you first to make plans based on *who* you are and *what* you would like to do after completing your studies, even though your goals will probably change while in college. It is vital to choose the right institution, plan your finances realistically, and ask for your family's full support. Stop here for a moment to evaluate and record your needs and goals on the basis of who you are and what you want to accomplish.

Prior to reentry, our records would have read something like this:

Chudwin (entering with 70 undergraduate credits): Attend a university close to home where I can drop out without penalty for certain semesters or modules. (Thought I needed to continue to travel with my husband.) Complete education for a Bachelor of Arts degree. Study literature, but look into field of behavioral sciences. Tentatively plan on teaching after graduation. Sever ties as volunteer with community organizations. Choose a school whose credits are reasonably priced.

Durrant (entering with no college credits): Take a few courses at a community college to see if I can do the work.

Teenaged children in school all day. Husband involved in his career. Discontinue hobby courses at local high school. Quit job as a receptionist. Consider taking courses to plan for improved income and professional status. Total number of hours needed for Associate of Arts degree, sixty-four. Choose a school with open admissions policy, short commuting time, and low tuition.

How did we fare? Much better than we dared dream. Both of us earned Master of Arts degrees over a five- and ten-year period, respectively.

Some of our planning, however, was "hit or miss." For example, when we stressed location and price of an institution, we did not realize how the absence or presence of support systems, like *student services,* would affect our reentry. We neglected to investigate the availability of refresher courses, self-development courses, scholarships specifically designated for older students, and a club or other space where women or returning students could gather informally to exchange information.

Also, we tended to view our family responsibilities unrealistically; we began our college careers without our families' full support. Housework was still our exclusive province; travels got in the way; illnesses slowed us down. Problems at home that other family members could have easily handled still demanded our attention.

We learned from our mistakes. But we also learned from other savvy students. One, a mother of nine, appealed to her family on the basis that a college education, when completed, would help her get a job and pay for their college educations when their turns came. A former student, now employed as Director of Student Activities in a college, convinced his family that going to school *full-time* would hurry him toward a higher-paying job and more prestige.

Today, many colleges insist that mature students take part in career and education planning workshops *before* matriculation. You might even consider using an educational brokerage agency first. These brokers can help you make appropriate educational decisions. More than 450 informational services are listed in the 1980 directory of *Educational and Career Information Services for Adults* (available from the National Center for Educational Brokering, 1211 Connecticut Ave. N.W., Washington, DC 20036 at $3.50, including postage).

Students who enter college programs after defining their goals and developing reentry skills do so with a clearer idea of what they want to accomplish and how they can go about doing it.

The School for New Learning at De Paul University in downtown Chicago sponsors fourteen workshops each year. Students must provide elaborate autobiographies and draw up "contracts" with clearly defined goals.

At Beaver College in Glenside, Pennsylvania, a transition course is offered for college credit. It is designed to prepare full- or part-time students enrolled in degree programs to meet many external and internal problems. The syllabus for the course includes studies in self-awareness, good study habits, establishment of realistic goals, study techniques, assertiveness, and other important skills and attitudes to make the returning student feel more confident.

At Bucks County Community College in Newtown, Pennsylvania, a series called "Thinking About College" is offered to help prospective students brush up on reading and writing skills and to improve their understanding of mathematics.

If you are entering at the freshman level, or if you feel that you need special launching and support systems, you should consider a school with programs engineered for your needs. Meanwhile, you might begin by asking yourself the following questions:

1. Where am I right now in my life?
2. Where am I going?

3. What are the obstacles in my path?
4. What kind of education is needed to achieve my goals?
5. What will my life be like when I reach my goal?

It is far better to spend some time investigating your goals and sharpening your skills than to begin totally unprepared, even bewildered. In the long run, it is the best defense against the misuse of your time and money.

3

Types of Educational Experiences

There are many paths to the top of the mountain. You can take the journey by way of night school, daytime classes, independent study, media, weekend college, even college-on-wheels.

Can you dally along the path, or are you in a hurry to complete your education? It is estimated that a degree in a *traditional college* will require seven to eight years to complete when maintaining a three-to-four-nights-a-week schedule. Although training in law, health care, education, agricultural science, and other fields can be accomplished as a part-time student, full-time study is suggested for degrees in the sciences, which otherwise could take up to ten years to complete.

In this chapter we will discuss traditional colleges and universities as well as new kinds of educational experiences that are challenging the familiar notion of a college education.

TWO-YEAR COLLEGES

Community colleges offer two-year programs for Associate of Arts and Associate of Science degrees. Usually sixty-four credits in "core" courses will earn your acceptance in the senior college or university of your choice, though more and more students are going to community colleges to get terminal degrees. In addition to college credit courses, community colleges offer programs that earn the graduate a certificate of skill in, for example, dental assisting and real estate.

You will find a good network of support among the 1,150 community colleges dotting the nation. Strong student development programs help you make career choices, brush up on rusty skills, and bolster the self-assurance so many reentry students lack. The majority of adult part-timers attend two-year colleges. Their enrollment comprises 61 percent of the two-year college population.

In the past, community colleges have been the poor stepchild of the educational system. Erasing the long-standing prejudices of some educators, these two-year colleges are now thought by many to represent the wave of the future. Since their mission comes from the message of the community, they can better respond to the needs of the community population, the eighteen- to seventy-year-old student. The City College of San Francisco has developed a special program that appeals to over-fifty students, who can attend school between 2:00 and 5:00 in the afternoon. Named the Matinee College, it offers a large range of credit courses designed "with the mature in mind."

Other advantages of community colleges are:

1. Cheap tuition and fees estimated at under $400 for a nine-month school year;
2. Open admission policy that allows students to enter with a high school diploma or its equivalent, or a minimum score on an aptitude test;
3. Easy registration procedures, sometimes done by mail;
4. Two-year career-oriented programs such as nursing, data processing, computer programming, labor relations.

Some people may not be as stimulated in a community college setting as in a university setting. There are no opportunities to take graduate level courses and the faculty members need not have Ph.Ds. However, it is a good starting point for returning students who feel less secure about their academic ability and career plans.

Junior colleges offer two-year programs for degrees and certificates. Most junior colleges receive funds from private sources, such as church and memorial funds, and indirectly from the federal government. Tuition is often higher and admission more selective than at community colleges. Whereas community colleges serve the local community, private two-year colleges lure students from near and far. Junior colleges have done little to attract adult students. According to a 1977 survey by the American Council on Education, only 11 percent of private two-year colleges have student service programs for older adults as compared to 58 percent of public community colleges.

FOUR-YEAR COLLEGES

Liberal arts colleges, many of which are privately supported and have small enrollments, offer four-year Bachelor of Arts programs that include disciplines in the arts, social sciences, sciences, and humanities. Each degree candidate concentrates his attention in a major subject area such as literature, music, mathematics, or biology.

Although the quality of the curriculum, teaching staff, and backup services varies greatly in the liberal arts college, it has one distinct advantage: classes are small and the opportunity to interact with professors, as well as counselors and administrators, is great.

Maintaining the goal of excellence in the face of declining enrollments has left the four-year liberal arts college particularly vulnerable. David W. Breneman, a senior fellow at the Brookings Institution, says it is possible that two hundred to three hundred small colleges may be forced to close their doors during the '80s.

Upper division colleges accept only students who have earned an Associate degree. Most offer junior and senior level undergraduate programs and graduate programs. There are approximately thirty such institutions in the country, concentrated primarily in Florida and Texas. The concept of the upper division college emerged about fifteen years ago to meet the needs of ongoing students from two-year colleges. Tuition is modest, the faculties generally good. Each is mandated to serve its own population of students. At a Midwest upper division college, Governors' State University in Park Forest South, Illinois, the average age of undergraduates is thirty-five.

Universities consist of many colleges operating under one administration, usually on one campus. Very large universities may have campuses in other parts of their home cities, in several cities (as with state universities), and overseas as well.

Four-year programs in undergraduate school and graduate programs for Master of Arts and Master of Science degrees are offered. Degrees in Law, Medicine, Doctor of Philosophy, and other professions are available in the graduate schools.

In addition to liberal arts colleges, universities contain colleges of business, education, and engineering, among other areas of study. The additional advantages of universities are numerous:

1. Most professors or department heads have earned doctoral degrees at top-rated universities in the United States and abroad.
2. You can pick and choose among the long list of professors teaching in your field of interest.
3. Library facilities are outstanding.
4. Fine museums and cultural attractions are often available.
5. Graduate level courses are generally available to undergraduates.

Don't be scared off by the word *university*. Some are providing superior services in counseling and support services for the returning student. The degree of support appears to be in direct proportion to the prestige and financial needs of the institution. When the pinch is felt, even prestigious universities look toward the adult learner with beckoning eyes. However, the most elite schools have been slower to follow this trend, usually in an attempt to preserve the uniqueness of their prized diplomas. Here older students may be rejected for three reasons:

1. The faculty is interested only in teaching eighteen- to twenty-two-year-old undergraduates and in the undergraduate experience.
2. Only full-time students are desirable as graduate and ultimately research assistants.
3. Older students' records are difficult to evaluate.

Some of these elite universities offer creditable evening schools. The University of Chicago, for example, has been offering a part-time M.B.A. program for forty years. It has the same admission standards and faculty for both its day and evening programs. It also offers a Returning Scholar Program on the main campus—*a nondegree program* with half-price tuition for persons thirty-five and older. If you hope to gain access to the university as a formal student, forget it. Over the last seven years only twenty-five of one thousand students enrolled in the Returning Scholar Program have gained formal entry through this route. Nevertheless, you can take seminars with eminent critics and writers, historians and scientists, and bask in the glory of the university's forty-two Nobel Prize winners.

Across town is one of Chicago's large public universities. Typical of many such urban educational institutions, the University of Illinois at Chicago Circle, with its 20,000 students, is located in the center of the city. It is an austere-appearing commuter school whose entrance requirements are lower than that of the parent school 150 miles away. The student body consists of a large number of blacks, foreign students, older students, and first-generation-in-college American youngsters who are working their way up the ladder of success. Ninety percent live in the Chicago Metropolitan area. It is an excellent example of similar urban-based universities.

Good support services are offered here, where many students work and "stop-out" for a term, foreign students brush up on English comprehension, and students of flawed public school training tool up on basic skills. Twenty-seven percent of the student body are part-timers. The office of student affairs also provides counseling for personal, academic, and social problems (even long-term psychological help). In their ombudsman role, they often help solve bureaucratic problems and offer emergency financial assistance. The university, which has traditionally been a place where new ideas are generated, where new experiments are tried, has extended that concept to help the ever increasing mixture of new students.

Yet the faculty remains steady, with such luminaries as John Fredrick Nims, poet, and editor of *Poetry* magazine; and Charles Rhodes, physicist and laser researcher. The campus is safe (the security record is excellent). And as one dean boasts, "Our best students here are as good as any 'best' students anywhere."

If your problem is distractions that interfere with study, you might want to investigate our nation's most northern university, the University of Alaska in the city of Fairbanks. Here winter temperatures drop as low as −60 degrees F.; together with winter's short days, this provides a strong incentive to study. To prove the point, almost half the population of Fairbank's 26,000 residents attend some course during the academic year.

As would be expected, in addition to traditional courses, the university is a center for research for wildlife, parks, and marine and geophysical studies. The institute of Arctic Biology has a special field site near Mount McKinley National Park, an alpine tundra station, and a reindeer facility at Nome.

Tuition is very low, and it is only fair to say that temperatures during the summer school session range in the eighties.

NONTRADITIONAL EDUCATION

New opportunities in education clear the way for adults who have been stymied from pursuing further education because of cost, lack of time, home and job responsibilities. Queensborough Community College is offering courses for credit at the Fresh Meadows, New York, branch of Bloomingdale's Department Store. The University of Mid-America, which has no campus, broadcasts courses into more than four thousand students' homes each day. Adult learning programs involve every topic, appear in all locations, utilize every means and almost every major agency in America.

Following are descriptions of some major types of nontraditional programs. For a complete listing consult *The New York Times Guide to Continuing Education in America*, edited by Frances C. Thomson (Quadrangle Books) or *Guide to Alternative Colleges and Universities*, by Wayne Blaze and Associates (Beacon Press).

The University Without Walls (UWW) program gives you the chance to earn a degree without attending classes at the university. Under the guidance of a faculty member or mentor, you can receive a graduate or undergraduate degree through a sponsoring university.

Thirty-one institutions of higher learning are involved in the UWW program, with headquarters at Antioch College, Yellow Springs, Ohio 45387. A maximum of twenty-four credits may be granted to you for practical experiences in fields such as accounting, journalism, art, business administration, practical nursing, and many other fields. In some cases, you can receive additional credits through the CLEP tests (College Level Examination Program).

Previously earned credits from college attendance may be transferred into the UWW program and applied toward your degree. Although you may have to attend the university to take some examinations, to do research, or to consult with your advisor, most of the work toward your degree will be earned through independent study. *The External Degree Program is offered in New York, New Jersey, California, Ohio, Illinois, Florida, West Virginia, Pennsylvania, and Connecticut and may be extended to other states in the near future.*

TV colleges are popular with at-home viewers in states all across the country. If you are tied in at home or geographically remote from college campuses, you can go to school without leaving the comfort of your favorite chair. Courses are available for college credit that will lead to a Bachelor's degree or an Associate degree in the Arts and Sciences. Courses are usually aired in the early morning hours on major networks and consist of lectures, reading assignments, examinations, and seminars. You may have to take several trips to the home college to register, buy books, or take examinations. However, many colleges offer all services by mail or phone. Credit cards can be used to pay for tuition, fees, registration, and book payments.

Correspondence schools or college-by-mail schools offer home study courses for college credit. Although you may not earn a *degree* through the correspondence school program, you can earn credits in a vast number of fields in undergraduate school. Graduate credits are also included in correspondence school courses; both schools are operated through the College Extension Divisions of sponsoring colleges and universities.

Most colleges will limit the number of credits you can earn through independent study. Extension courses, however, award students with graduate and undergraduate degrees, can be used for prerequisites for college courses, and can prepare you for CLEP tests (College Level Examination Program). For additional information, write the National University Extension Association, 1 Du Pont Circle, Washington, DC 10036.

College-On-Wheels is a new concept in bringing the college classroom to the students. This unusual college program is offered by Adelphi University to the commuters on the Long Island Railroad Main Line and on the Connecticut Branch. On the 7:00 A.M. train from the Smithtown area, classes A and B are offered three days a week. On the return trip from Manhattan to Long Island, classes C and D are given on alternate days. Although most of the students are working for M.B.A. degrees, some members are in undergraduate school. This is a degree program, and commuter students are able to make excellent use of their time on the long ride into the Big Apple.

The Elderhostel Programs encourage older students to attend classes at universities during the summer months. Nearly 20,000 persons over age sixty are participating on more than 300 campuses. Although it is not for college credits, we mention it here because it is an exciting adventure for senior adults. Through this excellent program, you can know the joy of learning while living on a beautiful campus. *All* the services available to students during the normal academic year are made available to senior summer students dedicated to the lifetime learning philosophy. In addition, you can stay in the dormitories, eat in the cafeterias, attend concerts, swim in the pools, browse in the libraries, and shop in the bookstores. Registration and tuition can run as high as $220 per person and as little as $20, but books and transportation are not included. More information can be found in your local library, or you can write Elderhostel, 100 Boylston St., Suite 200, Boston, MA 02116.

Radio and newspaper programs are an addition to the media college system that give students the chance to earn college credits at home, commuting by public transportation or riding in a car. These programs are especially popular in rural areas of the country where the closest college could be too far away to attend on a regular basis. However, urban commuters and people confined in institutions or at home have just as much to gain from this convenient college program. Phone your local radio station or newspaper office to ask if there is an outreach program operating in your area.

Weekend college programs offer crash programs for adults who are in a hurry to complete work for degrees or certificates. They afford excellent opportunities for working adults who are too busy during the workweek. Courses usually start on Friday evening and run through Sunday afternoon. At the undergraduate level, courses are offered in business mathematics, literature, composition, typing, drafting, history, and many other subjects. Although some colleges may have weekend accommodations for students who want to stay on campus, most students attend classes while commuting from their homes.

Cooperative education and work study programs have one thing in common. These programs give students the opportunity to complete their educations while earning money.

The cooperative education program is available to students of all ages who have completed the freshman year and have good academic standing. This program is active in both two-year and four-year institutions of higher learning. The cooperative education program that leads to the Bachelor's degree, however, takes five years. In the co-op program, the student spends six months on full-time campus-based study, with the remaining six months spent in full-time employment in work that is related to academic study. This program is open to returning students at more than 1,100 community or two-year colleges and senior colleges and universities throughout the country. It is sponsored by hundreds of businesses, corporations, and the government. Work experience must be evaluated and the student receives a grade; in most cases, credit is also given.

At Drexel University in Philadelphia, Pennsylvania, the co-operative education program is open to students in engineering, fashion design, home economics, business, and other fields. Similar programs are offered at Illinois Institute of Technology in Chicago, Illinois; the University of

South Florida in Tampa, Florida; and the University of the Pacific in Stockton, California.

Work-experience education or cooperative education programs provide funds while learning, practical experience in the field of interest, and an opportunity to test career goals. For additional information, write to Dr. Jim Wilson, The National Commission for Cooperative Education, Northeastern University, Boston, MA 02125.

Work-study programs are also advantageous in providing funds while learning. However, work and study are *parallel* in that students spend part of their time in class and part of it working. Work-study students usually are drawn into the program through financial need, and employment is part of their financial aid package.

4

Investigating Schools

As an education consumer, you have certain consumer rights: the rights to be informed, to be heard, and to choose. The wise consumer will compare prices, look for quality, compare brands, look for reputable dealers, and when in doubt, consult the Better Business Bureau. Apply these rights and principles to your college shopping.

Recession and double-digit inflation in the '70s put U.S. colleges and universities through a rugged preparation for the financial challenges of the present decade. As aptly stated by one reporter, "Snake-oil salesmen they aren't, but U.S. colleges and universities are learning the fine art of the hard sell."

A growing number of colleges are pulling out all the stops in the response to years of rapid growth of the two-year community college. Enrollment in them has soared from 66,000 students in 1960 to more than 4.3 million today. Four-year institutions are wasting no time or effort in their new courtship of adult learners. Here are some of their tactics:

- Barnard College in New York City, capitalizing on its location, put the Big Apple design on T-shirts and tote bags. They also spent $62,000 for mailings and posters.

- St. Joseph's College in Rensselaer, Indiana, hired a Greyhound bus to pick up students in Massachusetts, Connecticut, New York, and Pennsylvania and drive them to its campus for a weekend, for only a $50 charge.
- The successful, former director of admissions at Brunswick, Maine's Bowdoin College was hired as a headhunter by the University of Santa Cruz, California, whose Board of Regents gave the school five years to recruit a sufficient number of students to justify maintaining its present faculty.
- The prestigious University of Chicago takes out full-page ads in the local newspaper and advertises on radio to recruit students thirty-five years of age and older for their Returning Scholar Program.

Furthermore, a decline in full-time enrollments and an increase of part-timers—between 1968 and 1978, part-time enrollments at two-year colleges tripled and at four-year colleges almost doubled—has caused severe financial problems for big-city universities. Since state-supported institutions are reimbursed on the basis of their full-time students, it takes three part-timers to take up the slack.

So far there is little documentation of any abusive or deceptive practices on the part of admissions offices, yet it is up to you to find out which college program is just right for you—and whether that college lives up to the image given by its glossy three-color brochure. Here is how to do it:

First, go to your local library and look through the catalogs available there. Study the admissions policies, college board examinations and scores accepted, course offerings, tuition fees. Find out if services are extended to returning students. Is there an Office for Continuing Education? Are Life Experience Credits offered?

Keep an open mind. You may be surprised, for example,

to note that state college costs are following the lead of private institutions. You might also see that financial aid will allow you to attend a school with higher costs.

Some returning students have poor information and inquiry skills. If the catalogs seem confusing, ask the reference librarian to help you. This could be your first experience in the art of research.

Next address yourself to *your own* specific needs. Ask yourself some questions about the institution:

1. Does it offer the courses I am interested in?
2. Is the location convenient?
3. Can I afford it? (Will my employer or other financial aid assist me here?)
4. Can I qualify for admittance?
5. Will I be a welcome addition to the student body?

Definitely plan to visit the colleges of your choice *before* you make an appointment with a counselor in the admissions office. Be sure to pick a time when other students are on campus. Stroll through the student lounges, the library, and the cafeterias. Browse in the bookstore. Pick up leaflets or brochures in the admissions office or in the lobbies. Talk to students about how they feel about the school, the courses, and the instructors. If you have an outside interest or hobby—music, tennis, writing—is it really served on the campus as advertised?

If the school looks promising, ask the director of admissions to arrange for you to sit in on a few classes in your area of interest. You can tell a lot about the quality and the seriousness of students in a short time. Note the age and sex of those in class, their intellectual caliber, their apparent socioeconomic level; consider how comfortable you believe you will be fitting into such a group.

Will you feel safe on the campus? If the college is located in a midtown high-rise building, are there sufficient elevators to carry students between classes or will you have to plan on arriving early? What about security in the buildings and on the grounds during the evening hours? Are the parking lots well lighted and are campus police in evidence?

Bookstores offer a font of information. Textbooks and additional reading materials for courses of study are found at the start of the semester in the college bookstore. By looking through the contents of books in your field of interest, you can see your learning life laid out before you. You can also get the feel of the conservative versus nontraditional makeup of the faculty. Is *Peanuts* required reading for a sociology course?

Even if you have no prior experience or background in higher education, have confidence and trust your judgment, decisions, and gut-level feelings in making your choice of school. A friend who recently returned to college to study art lived in the shadow of a community college and a new university, yet he traveled twenty miles to attend a private religious college with an exceptional art program. It was a wise and happy choice for him.

HOUSING

Older students, graduate students, the handicapped, married couples, and families with children are accommodated in special housing on many campuses. Some rooms and apartments are in urban high-rise buildings or dormitories; others are in smaller apartment complexes and private homes. On campuses in rural locations, ranch-type housing, townhomes, or single homes are available for students and their families.

If you plan to live on or near the campus, get in touch with the housing office to find out about special housing arrangements for older or graduate students. Often older undergraduate students are considered for special housing, but priority may depend on your age, marital status, family size, or the length of time your name has been on a waiting list. Apply early for housing, and send in your deposit when you have made a decision about the college you wish to attend.

Dormitories and Apartments

Single and double rooms are available to older students on some campuses. Entire floors are often set aside for upper classmen. At Indiana University in Bloomington, one floor in a girls' dormitory is reserved for older students who do not want men visitors. In another dormitory on the same campus, an entire floor is reserved for older students or seniors in undergraduate school. Graduate students are quartered in special dormitories in which the lifestyle is less hectic. Many students live in apartments off campus, and some are roughing it in trailer camps.

At the University of Pennsylvania, a single-room apartment (efficiency) in a high-rise apartment complex in urban Philadelphia is available to older students and rents for $1,196 from September through July. One-bedroom apartments for singles, shared with another student, are $2,037 for each student. Larger apartments that rent for $2,252 per term are available to families or groups of four students. Private dormitories are reserved for law and medical students. These accommodations are typical of housing at larger universities.

Family Housing

On most residential campuses, apartments are set aside for married couples and students with children. Usually they are inspected and approved by the university housing staff. However, don't sign a lease for an apartment until you have seen it. It could spare you from bitter disappointment.

At Rutgers University's New Brunswick, New Jersey, campus, four apartment communities are reserved for students and their families. Unfurnished units may be rented near the campus with laundry facilities on the premises.

At Purdue University's Lafayette, Indiana, campus, many students live in apartments and private homes in off-campus locations. In the Student Services Office, lists of apartments approved by the university are filed, and incoming students are given excellent assistance in finding places to live. Rents vary from $200 per month to over $450, depending on size, location, recreational facilities, and utilities. Bus services are available to the campus for 25¢. Some local motels cater to students, with room and board costs at about $2,000 per semester. At the Family Inn, a special wing is reserved for students, and all meals are served buffet style.

CHILD CARE

If the care of young children presents problems for you, you may want to inquire about the campus nursery school or child care center. Often staffed by students and psychologists, these centers provide care for a small fee. Most Head Start programs for preschoolers are excellent, and wholesome meals are served. Before you decide to use the campus child care services, however, you may want to observe the kind of experiences other children are having and how they respond. For additional information, you can write to the Child Welfare League of America, 67 Irving Place, New York, NY 10003. This organization offers a number of helpful publications, including *Guidelines for Day Care Services* at $2.90.

Great care must be taken in selecting child care service in centers and private homes away from the campus community. To be certain you know how to evaluate a day care service, get a copy of the booklet, *Checking Out Child Care: A Parent Guide,* by Joan Bergstrom and Jane Gold. It can be purchased for 75¢ from the Child Care and Child Development Council of America, 711 14th St. N.W., Washington, DC 20005.

While you are investigating child care facilities, you may want to ask about baby-sitting services for young children. Often students earn money by baby-sitting, but many parents trade off sitting services.

A SPECIAL CONSIDERATION: SAFETY ON THE CAMPUS OF YOUR CHOICE

We have already mentioned briefly that you should assess safety factors in high-rise colleges. In any school you consider, do not be lulled into a false security by pleasant ivy walls and the idea that everyone is a student or school official. At inner city campuses or where deteriorating neighborhoods surround campuses, safety may be a major problem. However, just as our nation is experiencing escalating crime, schools and colleges are not exempt from the trend. It is best to be alert to danger at all times. This is particularly true for women students.

Every campus has a security force. Don't hesitate to call on them for what you may consider even a minor problem. For example, if your door is open when you return to your campus apartment or room, do not enter. Instead call campus or city police from an outside phone and they will investigate. People tend to be embarrassed about asking for police help unless they are in serious trouble. Police officers ride around in their patrol cars and walk their beats all day long and night. They want your business.

In the event you actually suspect an intruder in your living quarters, call the police or operator immediately. Report: "*a home invasion in progress*" giving them your address, apartment number, and name. Repeat your address twice. By saying "home invasion in progress" you will receive the quickest help. Here are some additional rules to follow:

1. Always try to walk with someone you know or among a group of people. Don't come and go at odd hours. Walk purposefully.
2. Keep your keys for your car or apartment in your hand when you are walking home or to a parking lot. Keys can be used as a weapon, too.
3. Stay away from doorways or the sides of buildings where assailants may be hiding. Walk in clear areas

and avoid places where shrubbery is overgrown. Don't take shortcuts through wooded areas.

4. If a stranger tries to delay you, don't stop. Get rid of him immediately with a definite "No!"

5. Women should use washrooms in secluded areas only when other women are present. Stay away from all secluded areas inside buildings, especially on campuses with high crime rates.

6. Call security for escort service if you feel your safety is threatened at any time. Report suspicious behavior of strangers to security immediately.

7. Check the back seat of your car before you get in. Park near a light for extra protection. Be especially careful in parking lots.

Some of these rules are plain common sense. In emergencies, however, common sense often flees. Make a mental rehearsal of safety measures now, so your defensive reactions are more automatic when you need them.

5

The Big Step: Enrollment

Despite the dip in college enrollments, colleges and universities are still looking for serious students. Each school has its own admission requirements. Some schools have open admission policies and accept every applicant; more selective schools may take only one out of three. Your life experience and maturity could count as a plus.

Don't dismiss a school solely on the basis of its catalog information. If you really want to attend, go after it by selling yourself to the director of admissions.

In some selective universities, mature women may have a more difficult time proving their credentials. As one admissions officer notes, "Take a man who retires from the Army in his early forties—it isn't quite the hassle to get him in as it is for a woman. His twenty years in the Army are easier to evaluate than women's work."

Women, especially those who have not been out in the working world, can give the appearance of not being serious. "What hurts women is their appearance of dilettantism," says one school official at a private university, "their attitude of saying, 'something is most interesting.'" If women make only vague remarks or are unsure about their abilities when they approach the admissions office, they

28

tend to create a poor impression and leave doubt as to their potential, in the gatekeeper's mind.

We remember our own experience: we were totally unprepared to meet the admissions officer. We thought our desire to enter college was sufficient. Unsure of entrance and graduation requirements, and totally ignorant of the system, we somehow bumbled through.

A short time ago, while visiting one community college, we met a woman at the cash register line in the cafeteria who was thinking about returning to school. When she saw our briefcases, she became flustered, dropped her change, and insisted we go around her. Our briefcases obviously signaled to her that we were, if not professors, at least minor deities. When we quickly told her we were former returning students, her color returned to normal—a classic case of "housewife-itis."

The point is that for a visit to the selective college admissions office, you must maximize yourself in every way possible. They may not think that your record shows a "clean" background because you have attended too many schools, because your high school transcript lacks luster, or because a long time elapsed between your educational experiences. You have to show them something more: 1) You have done your homework about their school and its admission and graduation requirements, and 2) you feel confident that you can do the work at their institution.

If there is a returning student's program on the campus of your choice, you can view it as a statement from the university that it welcomes older students. Visit this office first and ask about the admission process. For other schools, it is a matter of studying the catalog thoroughly and talking to other students to gain knowledge and confidence.

Keep in mind, also, that for those of you trying to get into a prestige university, one-third less intellectual effort and energy will be expended to meet competition and expectations at a less rigorous institution.

Make your needs known. During your visit with the

counselor, get in writing all important information about tuition, fees, and other costs. If special courses are promised, how often are they offered during the year? Will they accept your transfer credits from the college you attended ten years ago? In your desired field, what percentage of students are accepted into graduate school? In new institutions, check on the accreditation of the program that interests you. A college may be accredited, though a certain program within that college may not yet be certified by the appropriate professional association or state licensing committee.

Get extra credits upon entering through Life Experience Evaluation Programs and The College Level Examination Program (CLEP). You can hurry your way along by utilizing these two newest ways to accumulate credits without classes. Not every institution offers the option of Life Experience Credits. If they do, the experiences that merit credit may surprise you.

Life Experience Credits: To discover your own potential, write a biography. Prior learning may have been acquired through courses given by a corporation for its employees or through adult education classes, through public service, the military, Peace Corps, and other volunteer agencies. Perhaps you have run for public office, you led a scout troop for a number of years, or you did the bookkeeping for the family business.

It is up to you to convince the proper officials of your specific skills and knowledge as they relate to your educational objectives. For example, computer knowledge and sign language might well substitute for language requirements in some colleges and merit credit.

Methods of appraisal vary, but most Life Experience college credit programs have requirements in common. Samples of written work must be submitted, such as published articles or musical compositions if those are your accomplishments. After providing the written documentation as well, you will be interviewed by faculty members or a special Board of Governors and asked to provide letters of recommendation from friends or employers. In addition, you may have to present a chart, sing an aria, converse in a foreign language, or display your speed in shorthand, depending, of course, on the kind of college credits you hope to gain.

Life Experience Workshops are being held in institutions where the nontraditional credit programs are accepted. However, after your Life and Learning portfolio has been submitted and your work is completed, it may take many long months before your credits are awarded to you. If you feel you have waited too long, ask your counselor or the person in charge of the Life Experience Evaluation if there is a problem.

One friend discovered that the instructor of culinary sciences in a community college was delaying the evaluation because he doubted her credentials and had not had the time to investigate her proficiency as a gourmet cook. Having spent many years working in the family catering business, the student prepared a very professional, delicious selection of hors d'oeuvres and brought them to a Christmas party in one of his classrooms. Her credits arrived soon afterwards.

In another case, a returning veteran waited four months for his Life Experience Evaluation to be completed. He was informed that one professor, who doubted the value of nontraditional creditation, was holding up his approval for credits in photojournalism. Having worked in the Navy for a service publication, the veteran brought his camera to the university's commencement exercises and took pictures of the professor giving a speech. When the pictures and a well-written article were received by the professor, he quickly approved the veteran's credits.

The Life Experience program and other nontraditional learning principles are not totally approved or accepted in the academic world. Conservative or traditional institutions may look askance at your degree earned in such a fashion. This stigma may cause you embarrassment in the future if you apply to a graduate school in such a university. Employers may also be less than enthusiastic about special evaluation and life experience accreditation. Although the program is gaining acceptance in some formerly conservative circles, many academicians still feel that abuses in granting credits amount to a scandal. Others feel that Life Experience Evaluation is the trend of the future, that not all worthwhile educational experiences happen exclusively in the classroom. In view of all these opinions, you may be wiser to try to gain credits through the CLEP test.

CLEP: The second way to speed up graduation is through the College Board Examination Program tests. Returning students are encouraged to take CLEP tests to receive college credits for freshman and sophomore level courses.

Colleges recognize that adults have had educational experiences that are valuable. Through formal education, business experience, adult education courses, as well as through all forms of media communication, industrial training, and military service, adults have been gaining practical experiences that can enable them to test out of certain college courses. Because it saves valuable time with all students, "clepping out" of courses is very popular with underclassmen in freshman and sophomore years.

Tests are given the third week of every month at specified institutions called CLEP Centers, on two days for half-day periods and take ninety minutes for each test. You may take one test or several. Two types of tests are given: the general and subject examinations. Prepared by a staff of college instructors, the areas included in the general examinations test are English composition, history, humanities, natural sciences, and social sciences. The subject examinations are used to measure college level competency and achievement in *specific college courses* in disciplines such as business education, mathematics, medical technology, nursing, science, and social science.

If you want more information about CLEP tests, inquire at your local college or write to the College Entrance Examination Board, Princeton, NJ 18540. Registration must be completed three weeks before the test date.

A few people "clep out" of an incredible number of subjects. Here is one student's story. Denise L., age thirty-three, who had never attended college, returned to school in an External Degree Program sponsored by the State University of New York.

> Last year I made $26,000 in my own business, but I knew I couldn't make it farther up the ladder unless I had the credentials. After I was divorced, I met an old friend who was a counselor at a college and she directed me to the External Degree Program. I started in summer, took two courses, dropped one, and got a B in the other one. I still wasn't into it. (Within two semesters, I was able to work up to fifteen hours.) I decided to try the CLEP test and I was surprised. I took and passed the general examination in English Composition (three credits), the math general exam (six credits); I reviewed college alebra, which I took in high school, and got that easily. Then I went to the Winnetka public library and got a biology book, an old one, and supplemented it with a *Plaid* book study aid (published by Dow Jones—Irwin) to find out the latest information. I thought I failed that test, but I passed. I passed my tests in economics and finance too, but I failed accounting.
>
> I'm a good test taker. Somehow I know the answer from what I've heard, what I've read, or just by deducing the answer. Maybe I have to figure out what the answer *isn't* to come up with the right answer.

In explaining how she approached the actual test, she reports:

> I ask for a detailed explanation of how to take the exam and how it is scored. In CLEP, points are taken away for every wrong answer. I never touch my answer sheet until I go through all the questions. I write all over my question book. I read the questions, and if I definitely

know the answer, I circle the question. If I have to think too long, I skip it. By process of elimination, if there are two choices, I choose one. (I do not go to my answer sheet yet.) I cross out answers I don't know, then I check on my time. The first time through I count up the number I have right, for sure. If they are less than one-half, I go back to read and make the best guesses for the remainder. I may go back a third time. I go through my probable score. If I'm sure I passed, I stop and fill in my answer sheet. With CLEP you know in advance what your score must be.

Denise explains that she reads self-help books all the time. "I'm interested in discovering as much about myself as possible. I had a major illness in my early twenties. I thought I didn't die for a purpose. So I asked myself, 'What is my purpose?' I became my own person. I moved away and began my life."

It is possible that you may never CLEP out of exams to the extent Denise did, but her story of exam taking illustrates her tools for success: knowing what preparations to make, completely understanding the rules of the test, having a game plan, and an openness to trying the test. The total adds up to confidence.

Required Tests—SAT, ACT, and GED: We hope you are inspired by Denise's style because the more traditional schools will expect certain test scores. In addition, a high school and/or your former college transcripts will be expected. Your acceptance will either rest on these scores or they may merely be used as a guide.

The most common tests in U.S. universities and colleges are the Scholastic Aptitude Test (SAT) and the American College Testing Assessment (ACT). Let us consider the SAT first, which is given seven times a year in high schools and colleges throughout the country. A college or high school counselor in your area can tell you when the test is given and supply an application. The fee is $8, and you must register at least six weeks in advance. The results will be sent to you and to three colleges of your choice.

The test consists of two parts: The first is designed to measure your verbal skills—reading, vocabulary, and comprehension. The second part tests mathematical skills of problem solving and mathematical reasoning. Together, they take a total of three hours. SATs may be taken more than once to improve your scores.

The ACT includes four parts. The major subjects are English, social studies, mathematics, and natural science. The test questions are designed to measure your ability to relate intelligently in a college classroom. ACTs are given five times a year and cost $7.50.

Contemporary Books, Inc., Barron, and Arco publishers each offer books designed to help students become familiar with the kinds of questions asked on the SAT and ACT examinations for a modest price. Your local bookstores probably carry them.

Before the test be sure to get a good night's sleep. Arrive on time for the test or you will not be admitted. The content of these tests is well guarded, and to ensure the integrity of the exams, they are given at the same time across the country. When your test starts in Virginia, students will be starting in California.

It is wise to take a watch and several sharpened pencils with you. Also, be sure you understand how to fill in the answer sheet.

Take the first test in the fall of the year. Later tests within the academic school year will increase in difficulty to accommodate additional intellectual growth of students in the last year of high school.

If you don't do well on college entrance examinations, don't despair. Two-year colleges often have open admission policies. Some senior colleges require only a C average in lower divison work. There is a school for everyone.

GED test: If you have not graduated from high school you can take the General Education Degree Test (GED). Write to your state for particulars. Help is offered to prepare you for the tests through adult education and other programs. The test costs $5 and takes six hours of test time, which can generally be spread over a two-day period.

Orlando Stevens of Albuquerque, New Mexico, got his high school equivalency certificate at the age of forty-nine—thirty-four years after he quit school and ran away from home. He continued with his education and now holds a Ph.D. Adult learning centers, conventional night school classes, English (as a second language) courses, and one-on-one tutorial programs can all serve as springboards into higher education just as the high school equivalence certificate did for Dr. Stevens.

Educator and psychotherapist Carl Rogers states in his book, *Freedom to Learn,* that when a person "chooses his direction, helps to discover his own learning resources, formulates his own problems, decides his own course of action, lives with the consequences of these choices, then significant learning is maximized." In making your search and commitment to enter a particular institution you have already become a better learner.

6

Counselors and Faculty Advisors—What They Can Do for You

The field of counseling and guidance, which has in itself become a popular area of study, has generated a host of other helpful services. Let us take the time to study the kinds of advisors and counselors you will meet on campus. Your counselor could become your best friend.

When you enroll in college, a counselor advises you about courses, helps you define career goals, assigns you to a faculty advisor once you have chosen an area of interest, and assists you with personal problems. In many institutions these jobs are performed by separate counselors who may or may not have a degree in counseling and guidance but often do. Counselors generally are careful not to go beyond their own field of expertise.

CAREER COUNSELING

Typically, reentry students are going to school for something connected with work. One study prepared by the

University of California involving 1,042 adults found four types of adult students: those who had decided on a new occupation and were preparing for it; potential job changers who were attending school while examining options; career upgraders who were preparing for a promotion; and those who were broadening their education with a lifestyle change in mind.

For those who have already decided on a new occupation, it is relatively easy to plan both short- and long-term educational plans. Every graduate school from Harvard to the University of Wisconsin, for example, requires the same seven core subjects for the M.B.A. degree. Requirements for degrees in professional fields are fairly consistent.

For those returning to school who wish to make career changes, who have not worked before, and who are newly retired and are searching for self-enrichment or a second career, good counseling services are more crucial.

Typically, this group includes housewives, single parents who have returned to the job market and lack direction, and men caught in a midlife job transition. With goals as yet undecided, they must decide what skills they need to move up or start over again.

Many men and women simply lack the knack to assess what they were or could have been good at when they were younger. "We had to earn a living and took the path of least resistance," is the refrain. Something that was a hobby or avocation in the past may now seem appealing as a career.

Colleges and universities are beginning to develop solid career guidance services. Oakton Community College in Des Plaines, Illinois, has established an Adult Resource Center that offers academic and career counseling, vocational testing, and referral services to students and the community at large. Dr. Gale Grossman, a specialist in career counseling, helps students identify their values as they relate to work and what they would like to do in the future. "We focus on strength—what you are good at and enjoy," she says. "People are no longer willing to do what they don't enjoy. People also want to be more successful, especially women. They are no longer willing to settle for trivia in jobs; the media have changed us."

If your major consideration is to choose a field that shows continued promise of job openings, be sure to indicate this to your counselor. The U.S. Department of Labor and Northwestern University's *Annual Endicott Report*, widely recognized as an indicator of hiring trends, provide annual job and wage outlooks. As of the year 1980, for example, chemical and electrical engineers are in great demand, with petroleum engineers at the top of the list. Enrollments in engineering, computer science and technology, economics and business administration, sales, health, electronics, and energy-related courses are burgeoning.

These are only outlooks based on future predictions for the '80s. Job markets have a way of becoming saturated, sometimes without warning, as witnessed by the oversupply of teachers in the '70s and the poor outlook for doctors of medicine and dentistry in the '80s.

On more than sixty campuses Systems of Interactive Guidance and Information (SIGI) computer programs are used by counseling services to help students choose careers that accommodate both their professional interests and their personal values. To make their decisions, students ask questions and complete matching exercises. With this information the computer guides students to possible occupations.

In the early '70s, when we returned to college, good career counseling programs for adults returning to school were not as extensive as they are today. Consequently, we chose an area that was familiar to us, but which in effect offered us few job opportunities when we graduated. Perhaps a good counselor, knowing our interest as writers, might have pointed us toward business courses that would provide the knowledge that is absolutely necessary in the freelance writer's world.

Defying any planning or career decisions are those lucky instances of being in the right place at the right time. One forty-five-year-old, newly divorced woman returned to school to a women's studies degree program. Soon afterwards she switched from her job working for the manager of an export company to become secretary to the acquisitions librarian at her new university. Only a few months later her boss started working only half-time to accommodate a small child at home and she fell into the position of acquisitions librarian.

"The acquisitions department liked my business experience," she said, "and told me if I got my Master's degree I could keep the job. It was easier for me than for someone with a library degree who had no business experience. I knew about purchasing and advertising."

Business courses *do* appear to be the hottest item on the college campus today. Of the seventy correspondence courses available to students in rural Alaska, the one with the largest enrollment is elementary accounting.

A SPECIAL NOTE ABOUT COURSES

Despite all of this, put your well-laid plans aside for a moment and consider the following: you may never take the college route again, so this could be your only chance to sample a broad selection of educational offerings.

When we graduated, we thought we would never be able to leave the university setting, our place of intellectual rebirth. The fact was we did "cut the cord," as most graduates do. And although committed to lifelong learning, we will probably not return to a college setting unless we switch careers. So, we suggest that you take this opportunity to go outside your field and its course requirements to take an educational fling.

Ask a professor what "must" course he suggests students take outside their discipline and the answer is as varied as people's names:

"Women need to know about money management, credit ratings, and financial planning. Men seem to pick it up."

"Good writing and reading are essential. Writing courses are a way of getting to know ourselves."

"I recommend a personal awareness course that leaves a student with an 'I can tackle the world' attitude at its conclusion."

"Take a philosoply course and find your own philosophical base to operate from."

"To avoid becoming limited technocrats, choose courses from the traditional liberal arts program. Courses in literature provide us the best of Western culture. Problems about the breadth and depth of our lives are not ostensibly different from those that confronted people who have lived before us."

Derke Bok, president of Harvard University, in an address to entering students, stressed the necessity of taking three subjects: calculus, statistics, and computer programming. "If you fail to attack these subjects now," he said, "you will find it increasingly difficult to find the time and the will to master them later on. And if you fail ever to grasp these basic languages, you will find yourselves cut off from any of the most important issues of our time or reduced to depending on others to translate in diluted form the material you will need to grapple effectively with these issues."

We do not believe you have to choose between Hamlet and Statistics; you can choose *both.* Our own education was heavy on the former. We wrote critical papers into the early hours of the morning. It was hard work; it made us think. But we had no calculus, computer science, or statistics. They are foreign languages to us. We are dependent on others to translate their messages.

Granted, the smorgasbord selection of courses boggles the mind. The need to take courses for job accreditation is pressing. Money and time make their own demands. Yet it seems to us that the skills of communication and computation are necessities. You may find the time and will to master them later, but while you are at your institution of learning it will seem a lot easier. If you must keep your grades high, whenever possible, take the courses outside your discipline on a pass/fail basis.

FACULTY ADVISORS AS COUNSELORS

Once you make a decision to enter a program and are accepted, you will be assigned a faculty advisor. If you are lucky, you will find an advisor who is just right for you, someone with whom you can communicate. Before each new semester, you may consult with your advisor about course selections. At this time, it is also wise to bring up problems you may be having with curriculum, professors, and even nonacademic things like the conditions in the building.

One thing we looked for in advisors was availability. Note the fact that counselors who are members of the administration work a full day, whereas faculty members who are your advisors are not necessarily on campus for more than half of any working day. A recent study of a California university conducted by the Institute of Research in Social Behavior in Oakland, showed that although faculty members worked 60 hours or more each week, only 11.8 hours were spent in direct contact with students. The remainder of the time was spent in research and creative activity (23 hours) and university services (12 hours). If a faculty advisor keeps skimpy student visiting hours or frequently misses appointments, posting notes of last-minute changes on his office door, find a new advisor.

Advisors may be your major link to academia. They can become your mentors as well, write letters of recommendation, or let you in on new projects and research assistantships. If you are not satisfied with the advisor assigned to you, ask for a change. One student relates being placed with a faculty advisor for graduate school whom he had disliked as his instructor in undergraduate school. He asked the head of the department for a change and got it. "Under the new advisor," he stated, "I got some of the best instructors and most interesting courses."

Here is one final hint about choosing courses and advisors. Be realistic about what you can or cannot tackle. At one end of the spectrum is the returning student who needs to brush up on skills and should take advantage of the school's learning center—if one exists. On the other end is the student who speeds through school, eager to get into graduate level classes or out of them. "We're big boys and girls," they say. "Why can't we take them? We had these prerequisite courses in college twelve years ago."

"The returning student who is very serious wants to repeat the courses," says one administrative assistant in a large urban university's business school. "Women seem to be weak in math while men are weak in English, and you cannot function without either in business. Or they will come into my office and say, 'I want to be a CPA.' I tell them to take six hours of accounting and then see."

Even before you are assigned to your first faculty advisor, find out from friends, if you already have some in your future division, who the good advisors are. Often you can ask for a particular person and get him or her. *Ask* is the key word in all of your activities. You might want to ask the administrative assistant mentioned above if you can take an exam to prove your proficiency in a course you had long ago, then get a book out and study hard. The point is that it never hurts to ask. And making a friend of your counselors and advisors smooths the way.

7

Registration

The procedure for registration is basically the same at all institutions whose general student population includes returning students. Here is a list of tips to help you.

1. Decide on your courses as far in advance as possible. Choose alternatives in case some of your first choices are full.
2. Before you register, talk to your advisor, to professors you know, and to friends who have been around for a while about your selection of courses and the professors who teach them. Opinions vary, so get several. Teachers are beginning to provide detailed descriptions of their courses—teaching methods, grading systems, content—in course books. You might even ask to sit in on some current classes.
3. On registration day, arrive early to increase your chances of getting your first choice, although some colleges and universities assign days according to the initial of your last name.
4. Memorize your Social Security number.
5. After your program is approved, keep all program

44

information and receipts given to you by the university.

6. Recheck for clerical errors. Counselors and clerks get very tired on registration day and do make mistakes.

Some colleges have a policy of priority registration. When there is more demand than seats available for a course, graduate students and those who are about to graduate are given first choice. The Women's Reentry Program at Wright Junior College in Chicago offers advanced registration to allow mature students to schedule classes to fit their own lifestyles. Still other colleges use a newspaper supplement with a clip-out registration blank and course listings. A few even permit registration by telephone or mail and provide the option of charging course fees to credit cards.

And finally, if you are unable to get a course you want because of limited space, and you want it badly, consider going to the class for the first few days it meets and see if anyone decides to drop out. Most professors will be flattered at your interest and try to fit you in when possible.

8

Time Management

Crucial to success and sanity is the intelligent use of time. Everyone starts out with the same amount, but no two people's days are alike. Three hours a week in class requires, on the average, nine hours of outside study. If you took accounting before and you are repeating it, that won't hold true. On the other hand, if you have poor writing skills, it might take you even longer to write papers for an English class.

Students steal time for studying in unusual ways. One woman we interviewed went to bed at 11:00 P.M. with her husband, then rose like the phoenix at 1:00 A.M. to complete her homework without waking her partner. When Edward Lowry, a student at Temple University in Philadelphia, held down three jobs concurrently, he managed to tend bar and read at one end of it when business slowed down.

Studying and homework will only be a part of your day. As serious students, we found it most important, in order to meet all of our obligations, to become time and motion experts.

Begin by writing down on four sheets of paper the following: your family needs, your leisure needs, your work needs, your school needs. If jogging every day for forty-five

46

minutes is essential to you, list it. If growing a vegetable garden is not, eliminate it.

What can you change in your lifestyle? Can you eat off paper plates? Ask another father to take your son to Little League practice, explaining to him you are only temporarily suspending the job, not abdicating. Can you cut your employment to half-time after investigating financial aid at your school? Can you get up one hour earlier each morning?

You may think this is all clear in your mind; nevertheless, we urge you to write down your needs on paper and decide how changes might be made. It may show you that you are trying to accomplish too much.

When we returned to school, we stopped reading newspapers and instead watched the six o'clock news on TV. We shopped on weeknights instead of on weekends because the stores aren't as crowded. While studying, we carefully avoided answering the telephone. (If you are concerned about emergency calls from family members, agree on a special ring; e.g., two short rings repeated.) We learned to use the telephone to our advantage, saving steps and car mileage when locating gifts, furniture, clothing, etc. The time we saved with just the above changes was a minimum of ten hours weekly.

A further tip from our own experience is to avoid allowing friends to eat up your time by dumping their problems on you—if that has been your previous style of interacting with them. You needn't suspend your humanity. A bright smile, a warm handshake or embrace says you care.

Returning students, both men and women, often voice the fear that they are taking too much time away from their families. They are worried about being selfish in their demanding new role as students.

"There are many definitions of selfishness," says Elaine Sullivan, professor of student development and psychotherapist at Oakton Community College in Des Plaines, Illinois. "The fact that I have to set limits so that I can take care of myself and see who I am is not necessarily selfish," she says. "I'm going to do my own thing and the heck with all of you people—that's another kind of selfishness."

A middle ground needs to be found and this is always a difficult task. A lot of good communication between yourself and your family is the answer. Tell your family, "This is your home, too, and maybe I don't need to do all the things there are to do." When said in a nonthreatening way, this kind of communication can pave the way for spouse and children to help you develop control over your time.

One way to develop optimal understanding between you and your family is to involve your family in your school activities as much as possible. They will most likely have a positive attitude about your endeavor if they participate in the process. There are many things to do on campus: Take your children to the college library and introduce them to the children's literature collection. Or take your family to the concerts, exhibits, lectures, and plays offered by your school. Let them swim in the campus pool if it is allowed. Best of all, encourage your spouse to take some courses.

ORGANIZING YOUR PLACE OF STUDY

Some people study well with blaring music and family members in sight, but most students need a quiet place with minimal distractions. John Cheever, award-winning novelist, lived in a New York high-rise for much of his career and wrote his novels of distinction in a solitary basement storage room. Each morning he would rise, dress in a business suit, go down the elevator to his "office," change into comfortable clothes, write, change into his business clothes once more, and ride back up the elevator when he had completed his work for the day.

Your niche can be any place that suits you. No matter how modest your home facilities may be, you need a special place to study and store your books. This could be as elaborate as a room or home office or as simple as a corner of your bedroom or kitchen.

You will be surprised how quickly books and papers

accumulate. To save space and money, think about arranging two filing cabinets with a wooden slab stretched across the top of the cabinets to form a practical desk.

If you don't have space for cabinets, an inexpensive investment is a desk organizer that holds 8½-by-11-inch papers. Each section can be used for a specific course. Immediately drop all pertinent papers inside the corresponding slot, even if they are notes jotted on envelopes or matchbooks. Nothing is less constructive than spending time each day hunting for a scrap of paper with important information that you know you put "somewhere."

REGULAR STUDY HABITS

Try to establish regular study hours. "I learned something from my brother who is in medical school," said one community college student. "It was that if you don't study every day, you'll get lost. I study 2½ hours every afternoon for the three courses I take. I do assignments, review the material, and read ahead. On Friday I do a rough draft of my English paper and on Sunday I rewrite it. In order to do this I gave up my soap operas."

At first this woman's husband was not very happy about her study hours on the days when he was home from work. "He tried in every way to get me out with him by suggesting lunch or another activity, but I stuck to my plan and eventually convinced him of my serious intent," she said.

Another student reported it was impossible to study at home with his family. He made the library his special place of study to the point of using the same desk in the same location each time.

One mother we saw on campus brought her new baby to class with her. If the baby fussed, she simply lifted her blouse and nursed it, hiding both the baby and herself under the fullness of her garment. We noticed her thus serenely occupied in the library, the cafeteria, and the gym in the months that followed. While fellow students were doing double takes, she was doing double-duty study time, and both mother and child seemed very happy with the arrangement. Now that's creative time management!

If you are careful to reserve some regular open time for those close to you, you can successfully insist that your study time is not negotiable. Explain that managing your habits carefully gives you more time to enjoy with them.

HEALTH

Take care of your health. Surprisingly, most returning students report that their health was excellent while in school. Many attributed this to a happy and stimulated state of mind.

Since sitting is a major occupational hazard for students, plan on taking a daily exercise break such as a walk during your business lunch hour. (While walking we solved some of our knottiest problems as they simmered on the back burners of our consciousness.)

Some students swear to the efficacy of vitamin C tablets and health food products. College cafeterias continue to improve on healthful menus and it is rare to find one without a long salad bar and lots of yogurt.

SLEEP

"Who needs sleep?" asks the energetic returning student who juggles job, home, and schoolwork. "It's a waste of time," he says, rushing from one place to another. Mentally the pace may be pushing him over the brink but he doesn't know it because of his excitement.

Studies show that short sleepers feel a significant loss in their ability to think. Experiments with animals have shown that lack of sleep produces rigid thinking and agitation.

Don't cut the number of hours of sleep you find necessary to maintain yourself. Instead, find out when your energy peaks during the day by keeping track of it for a week. If you are an early morning person or a night person, make efficient use of those hours, but make up sleep on the other end.

Nevertheless, despite careful time-management planning, you can and should expect tremendous foul-ups: your mother-in-law will be hospitalized, your financial aid late, your term paper mislaid, your car tire flat—hopefully not all on the same day. Find a good coping measure in advance. On those special dog days, we always put on our favorite records for half an hour or gave the whole family a popcorn break.

PART II:
FINANCIAL AID

9

Getting the Financial Picture

Somewhere out there may be your share of the more than $12 billion available through government sources to students of all ages. Additional educational funds are offered by universities, industries, organizations, clubs, and professional societies in the form of scholarships, grants, loans, and fellowships.

Finding financial aid is extremely complex because of the abundant sources, the strict eligibility requirements, and the rapidly changing conditions on the U.S. political and economic scene. The financial aid officer in the college of your choice is the only up-to-date source of current information. As a specialist, he is an expert on conditions, requirements, sources, amounts, interest rates, eligibility, and other matters, and can find the best financial aid package for you. You must be persistent in obtaining his total cooperation because financial aid offices are usually understaffed and their administrators overworked.

WHAT IS FINANCIAL AID?

Financial aid is money given to you to help you pay for

attending college. Such funds come from these sources:

- Federal grants, loans, and work-study programs
- State-sponsored student aid
- College-sponsored scholarships, grants, loans, and work-study programs
- Privately endowed programs sponsored by clubs, churches, unions, businesses, industries, and assorted organizations
- Awards for scholastic excellence
- Cooperative education programs
- Veterans' benefits
- Employment

WHO CAN RECEIVE FINANCIAL AID?

It is a common misconception that financial aid is offered exclusively to the poor, young, or bright students. This is not true. Financial aid specialists report that adult students are eligible for all government programs. So if you are merely thinking of returning to college and you are not sure you can afford it, your chances of qualifying for financial aid are extremely good. Don't rule out colleges that have high tuition, fees, or other expensive services, either.

ESTIMATING COSTS

If you are still college shopping, speak to the financial aid officer at the college you are considering, but don't sign anything until you are certain of your choice.

If you qualify for aid, the total amount you receive will be the difference between the cost of attending college and the amount you can contribute from your own resources. In other words, this figure will be considered your specific financial need.

To estimate the amount you will need, you should first make a decision about the course of study you want to pursue. Next, select a few colleges of your choice. To calculate the cost of attendance at each school, *make a list of your personal income and assets, including your spouse's income and assets. List your personal expenses as a student: tuition, fees, books, supplies, living costs, transportation, and unusual costs such as child care or medical expenses.*

To reach an approximation of your financial need, estimate how much you can afford to contribute toward your education and deduct that amount from the total costs for each college you have selected. The sums remaining in each case will be the amounts you may receive in financial aid.

DETERMINING YOUR STATUS—APPLYING FOR AID

If you are currently enrolled as a returning student and you are not receiving financial aid, it is probably in your best interest to apply at the financial aid office. As a single or self-supporting student, you may be eligible for some type of assistance if your annual income is less than $6,000, if you are unemployed, or if you are receiving public assistance. If you are married or have dependent children, your eligibility will be based on your income while you are a student and your living and college expenses.

As we have stated, eligibility for financial aid is based on need, but other factors relating to your financial income are considered as well. If you are enrolled in a half-time schedule, you may be eligible for a Guaranteed Student Loan without displaying need. If you are financially dependent on a family income of less than $30,000, you may still be eligible for some type of financial aid. Apply for aid at least once to determine your status as a returning student. Additional opportunities for assistance are becoming available as we write.

HOW TO APPLY

The first step in your search for financial aid is to seek

the assistance of an aggressive counselor or financial aid officer. You may be required to fill out both the Financial Aid Form (FAF) and the ACT Family Financial Statement. Complete and return all necessary forms as soon as you can. *Time is extremely important.* Financial aid is anticipated by many needy students and they should be aware that the deadlines are strict. It is wise to apply well in advance of your return to college if you have a choice. If you fail to get aid this year, try again. Applications are available at the financial aid office at your college, at public libraries, and at U.S. post offices.

YOUR FINANCIAL AID PACKAGE

Your financial aid officer is in a position to design a financial aid package to correspond with your individual needs. Your package may consist of more than one of the following: scholarships, grants, loans, or work-study employment.

Preference for financial aid is given to students in degree or certificate programs and students maintaining full-time or half-time schedules. However, because of the recent overwhelming increase in enrollment of adult part-time students, more colleges are making funds available to returning students who devote less than half-time (less than six hours) to college.

10

Types of Financial Aid Available

Many types of aid are available to you once you have established your eligibility. In most cases, you are not required to submit a separate application for each type of aid. Once you have been admitted as a student and you have completed your FAF and other required forms, you may be considered for *all* types of aid.

Grants and scholarships have one attractive feature: they are outright gifts—free, no pay back. Sources include the federal government, state agencies, professional and service organizations, private foundations, and individual colleges and universities.

Loans may be obtained from the federal government through the college or university in which you are enrolled or plan to enroll. You may also negotiate a private loan through a bank or lending institution.

Work-study and cooperative education programs make it possible for students to earn money while attending college. Employment is often available in areas related to the field of study or academic interest. Wages for work-study employees are subject to variation according to the skill or practical experience of the student; payment is based on federal minimum wage scales.

Veterans' education assistance (G.I. Bill) provides funds for eligible veterans who wish complete education plans in colleges, universities, secondary schools, and training schools. Financial benefits escalate according to the number of dependents the veteran supports and the number of hours he is enrolled in classes.

Educational assistance for dependents of veterans who are disabled, missing-in-action, or deceased is also made available by the federal government through the G.I. Bill.

Employee refund programs for college tuition are sponsored by corporations, businesses, unions, and the federal government for employees who wish to return to school. Reimbursement is made for courses of study approved by the sponsoring organization only after the work has been completed and a grade of C or above has been earned.

GRANTS

If your financial need is great, your chances of receiving a grant are very good. Again, the most attractive thing about grants is that they are gifts. In addition to a grant, you may also be offered employment or be given a loan to meet your total college bills. To maintain a grant, your academic progress should be steady. Reapplication should be made *in advance* for each academic year, or you may stand the chance of losing it.

Although the number and kinds of grants for mature students may be limited at this time, several types of grants are given to all students whose need has been established.

Basic Grants

The Basic Educational Opportunity Grant Program (BEOG). These grants are sponsored by the federal government. The amount of money available changes each year, but the current range is from $500 to $1,800 a year. You may apply for the BEOG by completing the FAF, the Family Financial Statement (FFS), or the Basic Educational Opportunity Grant application (BEOG); residents of California may file the Student Aid Application for California, and Pennsylvanians may use the Pennsylvania Higher Education Assistance Application (PHEAA). You can obtain BEOG forms at schools, public libraries, and often at U.S. post offices, university financial aid offices, by writing to the U.S. Department of Education, Basic Educational Opportunity Grant Program, P.O. Box 84, Washington, DC 20044, or by calling the toll free number, 800-638-6700. The grant application must be received before the final date published on the BEOG form, but send yours as soon as possible. The deadline may be set by your school. *Apply early!*

At this time, you can qualify for a basic grant if you meet all the requirements listed on the application:

- You do not have a Bachelor's degree.
- You are a citizen or an eligible noncitizen.
- Your school and your program of study are eligible.
- You will be attending school at least half-time (six or more hours).

Supplemental Educational Opportunity Grants (SEOG). These grants are awarded by the federal government to undergraduate students who display exceptional financial need and who are enrolled in at least half-time programs. Currently the amounts awarded range from $200 to $1,500 with a maximum of $4,000 for a four-year program or $5,000 for a five-year program. SEOG funds must be matched or exceeded by other approved financial aid programs such as scholarships, loans, grants, and work-study arrangements. To apply, you must fill out one of the student aid applications. Contact the financial aid officer in your college to find out which one to complete. Usually, it will be one of the forms mentioned in the beginning of this chapter.

Foundation Grants

An excellent reference book is *The Foundation Grants to Individuals,* edited by Carol M. Kurzig, and published by The Foundation Center, Columbia University Press, 1979. This excellent source lists foundations that give grants to individuals. In spite of the fact that the Tax Reform Act of 1969 discouraged giving in this area, a surprising number of foundation programs still exist. The Foundation Center offers another publication, *Foundation Fundamentals,* also by Carol M. Kurzig, at $4.95. Send for it at the Foundation Center, 888 7th Avenue, New York, NY 10106, or call (212) 975-1120.

SCHOLARSHIPS

It is impossible to list the thousands of scholarships available to students in higher education, but we will mention a few. The best source of information is the reference room at your library, where you will find many publications that list scholarships, grants, fellowships, and loans.

The state in which you live has a scholarship program provided by legislative enactment, by the American Legion, by private foundations, by memorial funds, and by organizations; scholarships are also available to students of Indian extraction. See the list of state scholarship departments at the end of this section for addresses.

Scholarship funds are also offered to qualified students by fraternal, religious, social, military, and industrial groups. Being an excellent student is important, but there may be other qualifying factors. Many of these scholarships are specified for young people entering college directly from high school, but others do not specify age. Again, your best source of information is your financial aid advisor or counselor.

American Indian Scholarships

For students of American Indian ancestry, several agencies provide financial aid through scholarships and other programs. The U.S. government has annual scholarships for students of Indian, Eskimo, and Aleut blood who belong to tribes that are served by the Bureau of Indian Affairs. Other organizations providing funds for American Indians include the Daughters of the American Revolution, the Presbyterian Church of the U.S.A., the Lutheran Church of America Education Fund, and the Indian Health Scholarships Fund.

An excellent source of information about scholarships and other resources is *The College Blue Book, 17th Edition, Scholarships, Fellowships, Grants and Loans,* the Macmillan Company, Inc.

Funds for Women Students

The principle of "Loving Care" has been extended by the Clairol people from hair coloring to scholarships for women over age thirty. They offer them not bread and roses, but real hard cash to help them realize their dreams of rewarding careers.

Each year, $50,000 is awarded by Clairol to women students enrolled in full-time and part-time programs in undergraduate and graduate schools, with some individual awards as high as $1,000. If you are a citizen of the United States, you can show financial need, and you have a definite career in mind, you may be selected for a scholarship.

A booklet published by Clairol, *Educational Financial Aid Sources for Women,* lists other organizations that offer funding and financing for female college students. When sending for the booklet, ask about the scholarship program offered by the Loving Care Program. Write:

P. O. Box 14680,

Baltimore, MD 21268.

Money for graduate school is hard to find, but Sears Roebuck's Loan Fund For Women in Graduate Business Studies offers as much as $2,500 at 5 percent interest to women who are U.S. citizens, who are enrolled in accredited business schools, and who can demonstrate need. Loans are offered only to women in Master's degree programs and are repayable over a five-year period. Write to The Sears Roebuck Loan Fund for Women in Graduate Business Studies, 2012 Massachusetts Ave. N.W., Washington, DC 20036.

State Scholarships

Because it is impossible to list the more than 1,100 scholarships available through state offices of education, we present the list of agencies in each state as well as territorial agencies. Write to your state office for information about scholarships available to you as a returning student.

Alabama
Alabama Student Assistance Programs
State Office Bldg., Room 812
Montgomery AL 36130

Alaska
Alaska Department of Education
Pouch F (118 Seward)
Juneau, AK 99811

Arizona
Arizona Commission for Postsecondary Education
4350 Camelback Rd., Suite 140-F
Phoenix, AZ 85018

Arkansas
Department of Higher Education
122 National Old Line Bldg.
Little Rock, AR 72201

California
California Student Aid Commission
1410 5th St.
Sacramento, CA 95814

Colorado
Colorado Commission on Higher Education
1550 Lincoln St.
Denver, CO 80203

Delaware
Department of Public Instruction
John G. Townsend Bldg.
Dover, DE 19901

District of Columbia
Government of the District of Columbia
Higher Education Council
1329 E St. N.W., Room 1050
Washington, DC 10004

Florida
Student Financial Aid
Department of Education
563 Knott Bldg.
Tallahassee, FL 32304

Georgia
Georgia Higher Education Assistance Authority
9 Lavista Perimeter Pk., Suite 110
2187 Northlake Pkwy.
Tucker, GA 30084

Hawaii
Board of Regents
University of Hawaii
2444 Dole St.
Honolulu, HI 96822

Idaho
Office of the State Board of Education
Len B. Jordan Bldg., Room 307
Capitol Mall
Boise, ID 83720

Illinois
Illinois State Scholarship Commission
102 Wilmot Rd.
Deerfield, IL 60015

Indiana
State Scholarship Commission of Indiana
EDP Bldg.
219 N. Senate Ave.
Indianapolis, IN 46202

Iowa
Iowa Higher Education Facilities Commission
201 Jewett Bldg.
9th and Grand
Des Moines, IA 50309

Kansas
State Board of Regents
Student Assistance Section
Merchants National Bank Tower, Suite 1316
Topeka, KS 40601

Kentucky
Kentucky Higher Education Assistance Authority
691 Teton Tr.
Frankfort, KY 40601

Louisiana
Louisiana Higher Education Assistance Commission
P.O. Box 44127, Capitol Station
Baton Rouge, LA 70804

Maine
Division of Higher Education Services
State Department of Education and Cultural Services
State Education Bldg.
Augusta, ME 04333

Maryland
State Scholarship Board
2100 Guilford Ave., Room 206
Baltimore, MD 21218

Massachusetts
Massachusetts Board of Higher Education
182 Tremont St.
Boston, MA 02111

Michigan
Michigan Department of Education
Student Financial Assistance Services
P.O. Box 30008
Lansing, MI 48909

Minnesota
Minnesota Higher Education Coordinating Board
Capital Sq., Suite 901
550 Cedar St.
St. Paul, MN 55101

Mississippi
Governor's Office of Education and Training
University Center
3825 Ridgewood Rd., Suite 182
Jackson, MS 39211

Missouri
Department of Higher Education
Student Aid Program
600 Clark Ave.
Jefferson City, MO 65101

Montana
Office of Commissioner of Higher Education
33 S. Last Chance Gulch
Helena, MT 59601

Nebraska
Nebraska Coordinating Commission for Postsecondary Education
1315 State Capitol Bldg.
Lincoln, NE 68509

Nevada
University of Nevada System
405 Marsh Ave.
Reno, NV 89502

New Hampshire
Postsecondary Education Commission
66 South St.
Concord, NH 13303

New Jersey
New Jersey Department of Higher Education
Office of Student Assistance
P.O. Box 1417
Trenton, NJ 08625

New Mexico
Board of Education Finance
Legislative-Executive Bldg., Room 201
Santa Fe, NM 87503

New York
New York Higher Education Services Corporation
Tower Bldg.
Empire State Plaza
Albany, NY 12255

North Carolina
North Carolina Education Assistance Authority
Box 2688, University Sq. W.
Chapel Hill, NC 27514

North Dakota
North Dakota Student Financial Assistance Agency
Board of Higher Education
State Capitol, 10th Floor
Bismark, ND 58505

Ohio
Ohio Board of Regents
Student Assistance Office
30 Broad St.
Columbus, OH 43215

Oklahoma
Oklahoma State Regents for Higher Education
500 Education Bldg.
State Capitol Complex
Oklahoma City, OK 73105

Oregon
Oregon State Scholarship Commission
1445 Willamet St.
Eugene, OR 97401

Pennsylvania
Pennsylvania Higher Education Assistance Agency
Towne House
Harrisburg, PA 17102

Rhode Island
Rhode Island Department of Education
Office of Student Assistance
Roger Williams Bldg., Hays St.
Providence, RI 02908

South Carolina
Tuition and Grants Agency
411 Palmetto State Life Bldg.
Columbia, SC 29201

South Dakota
Department of Education and Cultural Affairs
Office of Secretary, SSIG Program
New Office Bldg.
Pierre, SD 57501

Tennessee
Tennessee Student Assistance Corporation
707 Main St.
Nashville, TN 37203

Texas
Coordinating Board
Texas College and University System
Box 12788, Capitol Station
Austin, TX 78711

Utah
Utah System of Higher Education
University Club Bldg., Room 1201
136 E. South Temple
Salt Lake City, UT 84111

Vermont
Vermont Student Assistance Corporation
156 College St.
Burlington, VT 05401

Virginia
State Council on Higher Education
700 Fidelity Bldg.
9 S. Main St.
Richmond, VA 23219

Washington
Council for Postsecondary Education
Division of Student Financial Aid
908 E. 5th
Olympia, WA 98504

West Virginia
West Virginia Board of Regents
West Virginia Higher Education Grant Program
General Delivery
Institute, WV 25112

Wisconsin
State of Wisconsin Higher Educational Aids Board
123 W. Washington Ave.
Madison, WI 53702

Wyoming
Wyoming Higher Education Council
State Office Bldg. W.
1720 Carey Ave.
Cheyenne, WY 82002

American Samoa
Department of Education
Pago Pago
American Samoa 96799

Guam
Board of Regents
University of Guam
P.O. Box EK
Agana, Guam 96910

Puerto Rico
Council of Higher Education
Box F, UPR Station
Rio Piedras, PR 00931

Trust Territory
Student Assistance Office
Department of Education
Office of the High Commissioner
Trust Territory of the Pacific Islands
Saipan, Mariana Islands 96950

LOANS

Student loans are very attractive because the interest rates are very low, and the repayment program does not begin until one to nine months after graduation from college or termination of your student status. Most repayment programs may be made monthly, quarterly, or biannually. Although interest rates are subject to change annually, the present rate on student loans ranges from 3 percent to 8 or 9 percent.

National Direct Student Loans (NDSL) are made possible by the federal financial assistance program. To be eligible for the NDSL, you must be enrolled for six or more credit hours each semester. Payment is not due until nine months after graduation at which time a 3 percent annual interest rate is charged. There is a strong possibility that this low interest rate will be raised in the near future.

A minimum payment rate of $30 a month may be arranged, but only if the entire loan repayment can be made in ten years. If the loan recipient is in combat service in the armed services or engaged in teaching the handicapped or disadvantaged, a portion of the loan may be canceled. The repayment of the NDSL may be postponed if the loan recipient resumes education, joins VISTA or the Peace Corps, or serves in the armed forces.

University Student Loans are provided through funds

supplied by friends and university alumni, industries, foundations, and civic-minded organizations. To establish your eligibility, you may have to be involved in an eight-hour program and present a cosigner for the loan. Although conditions vary at each institution, repayment of the debt usually becomes due shortly after graduation or termination. Repayment may be postponed if the student returns to school as a full-time student; joins the Peace Corps, VISTA, or Action; or serves in the armed forces.

Nursing Student Loans are available to students enrolled at least six hours in the nursing program. Funds are provided by the federal government and the university in most instances. Nine months after the borrower is graduated from school, a rate of 3 percent interest is charged on the unpaid balance, but postponement is considered for military service for three years, continued education, or service in the Peace Corps.

Health Profession Student Loans for full-time students in an undergraduate program in veterinary medicine or pharmacy are provided by the federal government and the university. Repayment begins twelve months after the graduate leaves school at a present interest rate of 7 percent. Repayment may be postponed for the reasons described so far.

Emergency Loans may be obtained through the financial aid office or the dean of students in the event of an unforeseen expense caused by a personal emergency. If you have an illness, a death in the family, or another special situation that results in a sudden or temporary lack of funds, you may receive a loan. Amounts very according to the policy of each institution, but the range is from $50 to $250. Because these resources usually come from a revolving student aid fund they must be paid within a short period of time.

Guaranteed Student Loan (GSL) is a loan made to you by a lending institution such as a credit union, a bank, or a loan association to help you pay for your college costs. The rate of interest charged at this time is 7 percent, but reports that the rate is on the increase persist. The GSL program is insured by the federal government or a state agency. The GSL is *not* based on your financial status.

As an undergraduate, you can borrow as much as $2,500 a year; as a graduate, you can borrow up to $5,000 a year. Repayment of the GSL begins about nine to twelve months after graduation or termination of student status with as many as ten years to repay your loan. No postponement policy is provided at present, but a deferment may be made under certain conditions. A premium fee may be charged by the lending institution in advance.

Health Education Assistance Loan (HEAL) is intended for full-time students enrolled in degree programs in the health profession fields. The loans are federally insured and are given for the following degrees:

- Doctor of Medicine
- Doctor of Osteopathy
- Doctor of Dentistry or Equivalent
- Doctor of Veterinary Medicine or Equivalent
- Doctor of Optometry or Equivalent
- Doctor of Podiatry or Equivalent
- Graduate or Equivalent Degree in Public Health
- Bachelor or Master of Science in Pharmacy or Equivalent

It is possible to borrow as much as $10,000 each academic year or a total of $50,000. Pharmacy students may borrow only $7,500 each year or a total of $37,500.

If you are enrolled in a health professions school that participates in the HEAL program, you may obtain an application from the financial aid office. Interest rates may not exceed 12 percent on the unpaid balance; repayment begins nine months after completion of your training, including internship and residency period, and termination of student status. Interest payments must be made on the loan while you are attending school. A portion of your loan may be paid through service in the National Health Corps.

WORK-STUDY PROGRAMS

The *College Work-Study Program (CWSP)* is a federally funded program and is administered by universities and colleges. It was established to give jobs to students in financial need. As a work-study employee, you can work part-time while classes are in session or full-time during the summer. A variety of jobs are available if you are eligible through the college or university where you are enrolled. You can work in the library, in the cafeteria, in maintenance, in security, or in an office; you can work in laboratories or as a teaching or research assistant, or you can do other skilled and unskilled jobs.

The federal government pays 80 percent of the work-study wages, while the university pays the balance. Full-time summer jobs are available to students who are in need of financial aid for the next academic year.

EMPLOYMENT

On-Campus Jobs

The financial aid office in most colleges can lead you to a wide variety of jobs both on and off campus during the academic year. Notices are usually posted in a prominent place near the financial aid office or throughout the school on bulletin boards. Like the college work-study program, on-campus jobs may be in libraries, student union buildings, or residence halls. On-campus employment has the advantage of closer contact with faculty and staff members and proximity to your classes.

Off-Campus Jobs

Getting a job away from campus on your own could be the best way to earn money to help pay your college costs. Earnings from tending bar and waiting tables include tips that can be lucrative. Housecleaning agencies generally pay good wages. Temporary help agencies can place you in jobs on a part-time basis with moving companies, in factories, or in offices. (One student reported having a job stuffing sausages in a meat-packing company, and another counted noodles in a pasta factory.)

Whatever you do, the rule is to work only enough hours to give you the funds you require. As a full-time student, a ten- to fifteen-hour work schedule may not endanger your academic record, but working longer hours could threaten your investment in school.

Employment while you are a student has benefits other than financial. In this way you gain practical work experience and increase your employment potential after graduation. In addition, you may also get firsthand knowledge of the limitations on unskilled workers which could make your desire for education even more intense.

VETERANS' EDUCATIONAL ASSISTANCE: GI BILL

As a veteran, you may feel the need for additional training or education to improve your career opportunities. The Veterans Administration program of financial assistance for eligible veterans has a time limit, so your benefits may run out before you have the opportunity to use them. A ten-year period after your discharge or release is allotted for educational allowances.

Hundreds of schools and colleges have been approved by the Veterans Administration to offer courses and degree programs for the reentering veteran to smooth his or her return to civilian life. Realizing that, in many cases, servicemen or women have abandoned or interrupted their educations to enlist in the military services, the federal government offers veterans generous assistance for education. The educational benefits of the GI Bill include pay-while-learning if you are entered in a full-time, three-quarter-time or half-time educational program or training.

Conditions for eligibility are determined by the Veterans Administration, as published in the VA pamphlet 10-67-1, revised March 1980, titled *Benefits for Veterans and Service Personnel with Service Since January 31, 1955, and*

Their Dependents. Some of this material is quoted directly, but we have added the numbering system to clarify and simplify the facts of eligibility.

1. "... a veteran must have at least 181 days' continuous active duty service, any part of which occurred after January 31, 1955, and before January 1, 1977."
2. "Discharge or release must have been under conditions other than dishonorable. This discharge requirement is waived for service personnel with 181 days or more of continuous active duty."
3. "A veteran with less than 181 days service may be eligible if he or she was released because of a service-connected disability."
4. "The 181 days required active duty does not include any of the following periods: When assigned by the Armed Forces to a civilian institution for a course substantially the same as a course offered to civilians; time served as a cadet or midshipman at a service academy; time served on active duty for training in an enlistment in the Army or Air National Guard or the Reserves, unless the person subsequently serves on active duty for a consecutive period of 1 year or more."
5. Educational institutions within the United States ... "providing education at the elementary school level or above may be approved for training. These may include public or private ... vocational, correspondence, business, or flight schools; colleges; universities; professional, scientific, or technical institutions; or on-the-job apprenticeship programs."
6. "A program of education at a foreign school must be pursued at the college level or higher. The Administrator, at his discretion, may deny or discontinue the educational assistance of any veteran in a foreign educational institution if he finds that such enrollment is not in the best interest of the veteran or the Government."
7. "Each eligible person with 18 continuous months or

more of active duty is entitled to receive 45 months of full-time educational benefits, or the equivalent in part-time benefits. Persons with less than 18 continuous months of active duty are entitled to 1½ months of full-time benefits (or part-time equivalent) for each month of active duty served."

8. "A person may use up to 48 months if he or she has entitlement under two or more programs (for instance, a person who has eligibility both as a dependent of a totally disabled veteran and as a veteran in his or her own right)."

9. "Veterans who have not received a high school diploma (or equivalency certificate) or who need deficiency or refresher courses prior to enrollment in a program of education or training may pursue these courses without charge to their basic entitlement."

10. "Eligibility generally ceases at the end of 10 years from the date of the veteran's release from active duty or December 31, 1989, whichever occurs first."

EDUCATIONAL ASSISTANCE FOR DEPENDENTS

"If you are completely disabled from service-connected causes, should die as a result of service, or should die while completely disabled from service-connected causes, the VA will pay up to $311 per month to help educate your spouse and each son or daughter. These payments are usually provided for children between the ages of 18 and 26 and their marriage is not a bar to this benefit. A surviving spouse's remarriage terminates entitlement unless the remarriage is terminated by death or divorce. In some instances, handicapped children may begin a special vocational or restorative course as early as age 14. Spouses and children of service personnel who have been missing in action or captured in the line of duty for more than 90 days are also eligible for these educational benefits."

At the time of the publication of the pamphlet 20-67-1, revised March 1980, funds to veterans in educational programs did not include a record of the most recent cost-of-living increases in payments to veterans enrolled in full-time, three-quarter-time and half-time programs. Because the funding for educational assistance to veterans is constantly being revised, both upward and downward, no universally true statement of present payments can be made in a book. It is best to seek the advice of an official of the Veterans Administration Office, either at the college of your choice, or by contacting the Administrator of the Veterans Administration Office in your area. The Red Cross also stands ready to assist people being discharged from the armed services in finding the kind of information you need to get back into school.

EMPLOYEE REFUNDS FOR COLLEGE TUITION

The federal government has led the way in subsidizing the educational costs of its many employees, and many corporations, businesses, and unions have followed by offering tuition refunds. In some business organizations refunds for tuition will be made to employees whose studies are in fields that would serve the business interests of the firm. A chemical company may refund tuition only to students majoring in chemical engineering or environmental studies. A bank may refund tuition only for students majoring in business administration, economics, or banking. Other organizations have a more generous attitude toward education and will refund tuition for courses in any field the employee chooses.

There are some restrictions, however, in almost every company's policies toward refunding tuition: an average grade of C is usually required, and the student must prove that his studies are not interfering with his abilities as an employee.

Often companies will advertise educational programs within the organization while downplaying the college tuition programs. You may have to inquire about your company's policies on higher education subsidies. You may also discover that your spouse can be included in the refund policies offered by your employer.

PART III:
COLLEGE RELATIONSHIPS

11

Starting Out on the Right Foot

Whatever your educational experience has been in the past, resolve now to make this one a successful and enjoyable one. Starting out on the right foot means developing classroom and study habit strategies that will boost your learning power.

Begin by doing a workmanlike job of getting ready to be a student. There are several things you can do before you ever enter a classroom:

- Go to the bookstore or a library and look at all the different titles, paying particular attention to your area of interest. Ask yourself, "How much do I know about this?" Start reading. Read a book or two a month. If you haven't read anything except newspapers for the last ten years, you can't expect to do the intensive reading of a text immediately. The words *college* and *textbook* become synonymous in the life of a student.
- For a fast start, get a copy of the course outline and text—even two months ahead. If your college book-

store does not have the text, other bookstores will.

- Learn to read a class schedule. "I didn't know how to read a schedule," says one community college student, "so I missed the first three class periods in chemistry."
- Sign up for a returning student seminar if your university or college offers one. You can always drop it if you find it too elementary.

NONVERBAL COMMUNICATION

It is estimated that as much as 65 percent of meaning in our communication comes from nonverbal clues. Each of us can discern the emotions and meanings behind facial expression, voice tones, and posture. We often give teachers the impression, through our nonverbal communication, that we don't care about their classes or even like them.

Sometime after a class has filled and before the professor arrives, stand at the front of the room and look at your classmates. This will give you a new view of your classmates' behavior—the view your teacher sees each time he interacts with the class. You might notice that one student is eating potato chips. Someone else is reading the newspaper. A few others are napping. And the situation doesn't improve when the prof starts the class. Suddenly the door opens and another student casually saunters in and crosses in front of the teacher to find a seat. The point is this: don't be an amateur student; be a professional.

Teachers interviewed repeatedly say they appreciate students with zest, spark, and enthusiasm. This can be conveyed without uttering a word by doing the following:

- Face your instructor with an interested look on your face.
- Establish good eye contact. Smile or nod your head as he or she speaks to show the professor that you are following his or her thinking.
- If the instructor tells a joke, give some kind of

response—a polite laugh or chuckle, even a groan
will do.
- If it was an interesting class session, smile and show
the teacher you liked it. In fact, stop to say so before
you leave.

It is unfair to expect someone who teaches a subject over
and over to supply all the enthusiasm. Returning students
can "speak" body language to help motivate instructors,
which in turn will make the class a lot more interesting.

WHERE TO SIT

We are creatures of habit and choose a place or area in
class that automatically seems to suit us. Before staking
out a claim to a particular seat in class, consider the following:

- Professors tend to focus their attention to the center
of the class and look left to right, then back again.
- Some stand at the first row and look over the heads
of students sitting in the first row.
- Sitting in the last row has a negative connotation.

What you want to have is good eye contact with the
instructor and be in a location where you can view the
blackboard and copy its contents without his back in the
way. If you concentrate on maintaining eye contact, and
throw in some head shaking for good measure, you will feel
as if you are getting a private lecture after three or four
weeks of classes.

ASKING QUESTIONS

By trying to answer as many questions as possible, you
show that you are keeping up with the material and that
you are interested in the course content. "There will come a
time when a particularly difficult question is going to be

raised," says the director of one university learning center. "When the prof looks you in the eye expectantly, you can shrug as if to say, 'I've been answering questions all semester. Lay off.'"

Try not to duck your head when questions are being asked. It is a clear indication of not being prepared. If you are called on and really don't know the answer, be honest and say so.

A good way to psyche out the kinds of questions a particular teacher asks is to role play. Pretend you are the instructor. Develop questions and answers from your text and the professor's lecture notes *before* you go to class. Then see how closely these questions and answers match the actual class experience. It won't take long to see if you are on the same wavelength.

Deciding how many questions to answer in a class period often disturbs returning students. They do not want to appear threatening to younger students or instructors by flaunting their knowledge or seeming overly eager. A good rule of thumb to follow is to avoid showing off and dragging in a lot of personal experience, and to answer as many questions as you wish without hogging the entire class time. You will not be punished for consistently volunteering to answer questions. In fact, you will cultivate more friends. Students always look for advantages that will benefit their own college careers, and will usually be drawn to other students who appear to be successful—whether they want advice, informal tutoring, or just your stimulating companionship.

Depending on your confidence level, speaking out in class may be difficult, even traumatic. The professor looms high as a figure of authority; twenty pairs of eyes are riveted on your face. Suddenly you feel your heart racing, your throat constricting, your memory fleeing—the classic signs of stage fright. You might try this strategy which was suggested by a singing coach who taught it to performers to relieve their jitters: apply opposing pressure to parts of the body—squeeze your hands or knees together as tightly as possible. This relieves the offending strain in the vocal chords, or wherever it may be. If this fails, try imagining your audience without their clothes (without laughing, of course).

THE SUPREME PLOY

Professors will respond positively to flattery. If flattery is part of your modus operandi and you use it well, you can not only start out on the right foot, but get in the side door as well. One prof tells this story. "In a course I taught, in which I gave four quizzes and a final, a particular student came in asking about his notes. We talked and talked. He absolutely charmed the first quiz right out of me. Before each quiz and then the midterm he repeated the process. He could have charmed a handkerchief from a silkworm. I knew what his purpose was. As much as I was on guard, my obligation to my subject matter and to him as a student required that I discuss the subject matter fully with him, even to correcting his notes."

In a sense there is some reciprocity here. Teachers do not like assembly line students. Everyone likes diversion. Everyone needs strokes. Even if you tend to be shy, try a little honest flattery of your professor. Professors sometimes do the same thing with students.

GOOD STUDY HABITS

Psyching out the professors and flattering them will only help if you are serious about your studies. Keep in mind that learning is especially important in the early units of a course. If you spend a good deal of time learning the material early in the term, you will have less trouble as the course progresses. That is why it is important to set up your priorities at work and at home so you are ready to start out on the right foot.

12

The Professor's Right Side, Biases, and Pet Peeves

For ecological reasons alone a lot of the professors—like the whooping crane, the alligator, and the adorable panda, none of which accomplishes a hell of a lot— should be preserved. . . . Most seek to recognize and reward distinguished accomplishment by their students. They still stand for the maintenance and advancement of high culture as venerably conceived. The fact that on their committees it is more important to talk about a problem than to solve it is not without some redeeming value. We treasure some rare birds for the song they sing.

Richard D. Mandell, from *The Professor Game*

When Lauren L. returned to the campus to complete his graduate degree in hospital administration at an Iowa university, he discovered that one of the required courses was taught by a gentleman who insisted students dress in jacket and tie and rise when he entered the classroom. Lauren laughed it off, but two of his fifteen classmates actually dropped out of the program.

A reentry student at a community college in the West reports that a tenured teacher at her school is so inept that the word is out to avoid her course at all costs. The students are constantly foiled by this teacher's crafty name changes. After marriage, divorce, a return to her maiden name, another marriage, and a repetition of the whole process, unsuspecting students found that whether she called herself Smith, Jones, or Green, the same face appeared behind the desk.

A return to school is certainly more than just spending a few years at another address. A return to school often causes a dramatic change in the kinds of people you must relate to, mainly that rare bird, the professor.

At the beginning of each semester, your life will suddenly entwine with those of your professors. Your brains will make contact; your personalities, or lack of them, will be displayed for all to observe. The radical teacher may be perceived by you as exciting and thought provoking, but by others as flaky; the teacher who frankly admits she can only relate to women will be seen as a threat to men, as a surprise to women; the formal teacher with his tweed coat and elegant manners will be judged as helpful by you, a cold fish by others.

Personalities vary on one side of the desk as much as on the other. Although this diversity sounds pretty overwhelming at first, all students have an obligation to get to know their professors for two important reasons:

1. The teachers serve as the intellectual digests of material in your subjects. They may be able to guide you to a more detailed concept in your area of interest.

2. By interacting and getting to know your professors, you may be able to improve marginal grades. The teachers may remember you and say, "Yes, he's on top of it. I'll give him an A." If you are simply a name and a series of grades they might decide on a B.

Teachers have very strong notions of how their students should act in the classroom and the attitude they should take toward the course work. Be glad if they inform you of this outlook early in the semester. Although you should not give up the essential "you," your existing multiple roles of spouse, parent, worker, etc. will make it easier for you to adapt to the idiosyncrasies of individual teachers.

Ideally, students should be judged solely on their knowledge of the subject, but ideal situations rarely exist. A good working relationship with your teachers—knowing what they expect—will lay the foundation for a positive experience. Six professors report here on six fatal errors students commit:

1. *"Thou shall not be a smart ass,"* says a teacher of literature. "Literature is important to me. Don't be flip about this subject. I am not going to tell a student why Henry James is important. The student must come to the subject. The subject does not come to him."

2. *Participating in chitchat and using class time to solve your personal crises* is disliked by a professor who says, "In women's studies, in particular, we get a lot of women with personal problems who use the class to air them. I won't deal with that."

Older women who have long been housebound, have been accused of applying irrelevant experiences to the class material. Some do. Others are afraid to speak up in class about anything. In our experience, the worst offender in this category was a newly retired army colonel whose patter belonged on a TV sitcom.

3. *Failing to contribute to the class throughout the term is a common gripe of teachers.* One teacher says "The helpful student—the talker that you can always count on to carry through the rough spots, one you can always count on to say the provocative thing or to answer the question that no one wants to tackle—is a godsend."

4. *Students who refuse to make any serious effort shortchange themselves, their fellow students, and their professors.* "The attitude that annoys me more than anything," says one prof, "is that they think the work is supposed to be easy. If I sense a student is lazy or just dragging, I come down hard. An excellent student complained that she had

gotten an A in every course except mine. Condescendingly, she wrote a lousy final exam and handed it in because she thought she could get away with it. Then she came crying to me about her B."

5. *Flaunting your knowledge will only antagonize your classmates—and sometimes, your professor.* If you come from the working world, where you have been doing a job for which you are now earning credentials, you should be careful how you respond to familiar material. You may think that learning about the price-earning ratio of stocks is Mickey Mouse stuff, but your twenty-year-old classmates might not agree. A statement like, "Don't tell me anyone doesn't know that," is tantamount to waving a red flag. If you know that much about the course content, try to pass it by special examination.

6. *Falling asleep is absolutely tabu.* It is very easy to see from the front of the room who is listening and who is dozing off. Although you may arrive at an evening class directly from work and feel tired, profs don't take kindly to sleepers.

— Teachers reflect a variety of attitudes toward dress, attendance, and exams. Anything short of a Halloween costume (when it is not Halloween) is appropriate with most. On the subject of attendance, the general attitude among professors is that you are big boys and girls who are paying for your education, and showing up for classes is your responsibility. On the other hand, teachers vary widely in their attitudes about late papers and makeup exams. This should be spelled out very clearly in the course syllabus. If it is not, ask early in the term for clarification, before you are faced with either problem. (One student was not admitted for a final exam because he was six minutes late to class. See Part IV, Chapter 21 for more information on this type of situation.)

The degree of formality varies from teacher to teacher depending on the department and the institution. In general, three systems of address are used between professor and students:

1. The teacher calls students by their first names; the students address the professor formally.
2. Informal address is open to negotiation on both sides as professor and student get to know one another.
3. There is equal informal or equal formal address.

From a prestigious university two professors comment:

Professor A: "I prefer a slightly more formal basis if only because I think it is better for the academic situation. I do call people Mr. and Mrs. in class, but here in the office it is generally first names (though not reciprocated by students)."

Professor B: "I call students by first name—even in classes of up to sixty. I tell them they are free to call me by my first name. Some do. All the graduates do. Of late, there is a tendency for women students to use my first name more readily. The older students do it more easily, those who are closer to my age."

Early in the semester your teachers will indicate which system they use. However, if you do not wish to be called by your first name, for example, say so.

The teacher's title often adds to the confusion in this situation. We have used the terms *professor, teacher, instructor,* and *doctor* indiscriminately throughout the book. Any and all of these titles are found on campuses. In one small university, a professor whom we addressed as doctor said, "Everyone here is a doctor or professor! Even the janitor."

At schools that rank their faculty, not everyone who teaches is a professor, even if he or she holds a Ph.D. A short history here may help you understand this muddle.

The Ph.D. degree was not offered in numbers until after the Civil War. At the turn of the century, at the discretion of the university, patterns of rank emerged—instructors, assistant professors, associate professors, and full professors. Only the latter were addressed as Professor. Administrators were distinguished by titles of dean, provost, and chancellor.

This tradition continues at many institutions, although a teacher may have a string of titles and degrees and still wish to be called Mr. or Ms. However, particularly at schools that do not rank their faculty, titles of Doctor and Professor are commonly and indiscriminately used, both because of confusion on the part of unknowing students and because of gentle sham on the part of knowing teachers.

It is not difficult to understand why teachers let students go on using the term *professor* inappropriately. Until recent years, college teachers have been on the low end of the professional's pay scale. A title to soothe the ego is at least some compensation. Further compensation is the American university's endorsement of intellectual distinction and the freedom given to faculty members to develop their skills and talents. Consequently, teachers have enormous freedom in the confines of their own classrooms to teach as they please, to interact with their students as they choose, and to name themselves. This freedom is guarded with the zeal of Circe at the gates of her palace. Woe to him who crosses the threshold and interferes.

The irony is that few college teachers have ever had any teaching courses. Each year raw new Ph.D. holders are plunked down in front of unsuspecting entering students with the simple belief that knowledge of their subject and thesis will somehow carry them through—and that all will be well in paradise.

Is it any wonder that reentry students are faced with a certain number of green "professors" starting out on the wrong foot who are threatened by older, more experienced students? Or that they may be faced with an odd professor whose Neanderthal habits are protected by the guarantee of academic freedom? Does it seem to you that professors have a lot of power in the classroom? Of course they do. They are rare birds.

In any case, don't worry unduly. The cast of characters will change each term and your teachers will largely be competent and fair. However, if you do happen to get a *very* rare bird and your options are nil, try to be a philosopher. Listen to his song.

13

Mentors

In Greek legend, Mentor was the loyal friend and wise advisor of Ulysses. In today's world, mentors tell you about the world, open doors to opportunities, and provide some kind of model for your behavior.

Some students feel the value of mentors lies in their ability to recognize special talents even before the students do. "I didn't see my advisor socially," says one woman. "But in terms of how you define a friend, he *was* a friend. He had my best interests at heart. He took me seriously—my ability and ambitions—in a way nobody else had, and he gave me a sense of taking myself seriously. I showed him my writing, and he saw something in it that I was afraid others wouldn't. He treated me as someone with ability and I started believing it."

Women, in particular, have been reading articles about sponsors and mentors in the business world, sometimes at a superficial level. *Mentor* is not just a buzzword. The mentor relationship requires great effort on the part of the student and the teacher. Since teachers are wrapped up in their own intellectual pursuits and opportunities in their own careers, it stands to reason that there are only so many mentors to be shared by so many students.

FINDING A MENTOR

First of all, align yourself with people who boost others. It will be obvious after a while that some people in high places who can give you a boost are just plain stingy. It is as if they were playing an internal tape that says that they made it the hard way and now you must, too. They may appear perfectly amiable, but in their hearts they are hopelessly unhelpful.

You will also encounter the people we call *limited mentors*. Professors or advisors who fall into this category might say, "I am subject matter–oriented. My relationships with my students grow out of that relationship. I don't think it's my business to be a guru." This nonguru will be helpful, even warm, in his relationship with you but the line he draws across his office floor, separating his desk from your chair, is impenetrable.

Finally, you will meet full-blown, 100-percent mentors who really take you under their wings, hold you tightly until just the right time, then set you free. These mentors direct you to special people, materials, and projects. They never allow you to feel they are put upon, and they freely share their expertise. A thirty-year-old returning male student reports the following:

> I became involved with a professor on a project. Mainly his value to me was seeing how he did something, how he went about doing his job, dealt with grants and his research.
> First you see a potential mentor in a friendly way, then you realize he has done well in his position. Perhaps he can help.
> Usually they take you under their wing. It is never said; it just happens. They don't feel threatened or taken advantage of because they are already your friends.

A more deliberate view in finding a mentor is expressed by students who insist you must deliberately spark a potential mentors' interest and appeal to them. "They have to believe you are worth it. You have to sell yourself," says an older woman who claimed that, as a student, she was fat, fifty, and a B-minus student, though she is now svelte and working as a professional with a senior citizen group. "Volunteer, volunteer," was her suggestion, as she recalled that she offered her time at her university's Women's Resource Center. There she developed close contact with a professor of women's studies who took her under her wing and eventually helped her find a job.

At the graduate and Ph.D. level, as your goals become more defined, a mentor can become even more significant to your career development. It may also be more difficult for potential mentors to focus on your problems and aspirations because they may now view you as a competitor.

GIVING UP YOUR MENTOR

Giving up a mentor or the opposite usually means that you have developed to the point at which you can manage your own life. With the passing of time, all things change. Just as you made changes to return to school, you now move on to other pursuits.

The idea of finding a mentor may seem unnecessary, even embarrassing, to some mature students. Most of us do not wish to appear helpless. Yet, in our fast-moving world, people do need people as never before. As anthropologists Nena and George O'Neill, authors of *Shifting Gears,* state, "With so many new options open to us, we may find that we need a new mentor at fifty when we embark on a new career, even though we have already let go of previous mentors and become mentors ourselves in some areas of life. . . . Thus choosing and letting go of mentors becomes a continuous process, just as our own lives are a continuous process."

Mentor relationships develop in academia because people who are able to help are turned on by certain qualities of enthusiasm, perseverance, and personality in the student. The student, in turn, shows a desire and appreciation for the mentor's attention. It is reciprocal at its best, a beneficial two-way street.

14

How to Infiltrate the
Power Structure

In a commuter school few people really infiltrate anything as far as the power structure is concerned. However,
they still have the opportunity to achieve identity and
develop skills outside their classroom work.

On the other hand, at some time in your college career
you are going to feel the need to get something special for
yourself, to effect a change, or to holler for help. Determin-
ing who has clout in your university or college is a helpful
exercise. If you intend to go into business, health services,
education, or a host of other areas that are institutional-
ized, academia will give you a good perspective of the
pecking order within a bureaucracy.

It takes about six months to get the picture, to find out
who really has clout as compared to who *appears* to have
it. In institutions that rank their faculty, the full professor
is a person with great power. New teachers have the least.
Assistant deans are often cloutless. In some schools the
registrar may have more power than the dean, and the
provost more power than the president.

How do you find out about the pecking order? Essentially
you do so by asking questions and by observing. Two

reentry women we knew went out for coffee with their professor after evening classes. In that informal situation, they gained valuable insight into the workings of his department.

You will notice that certain people are always being consulted, even by those in other departments. You will know when the vice-president for academic affairs or the Nobel laureate is in the area, because someone will always be talking eagerly to that individual.

Ask someone to get something done. If that person can't help, obviously you have approached the wrong individual. You must seek out the "powerholder," the person with the capacity to act and to effect a desired result by picking up the telephone or affixing his or her name to a piece of paper.

"I like to think of the university as basically anarchistic," says one political scientist. "There is an administration who thinks it has power but in fact has no power at all. The faculty does what it damn well pleases. It seems to me that the administration has power over matters that are not important. They don't have power about what happens in class. What's valuable is the education."

Faculty members who have worked as administrators as well are less likely to agree. For example, if the president or the board members of your university do not think an adult reentry program is important, little staff or money will be designated for this area.

MAKING INROADS

Cliff D. is a highly visible character on his school campus today. "It wasn't always that way," he said. "I spent my first quarter here being the typical student. And then the grade issue came up at my school. It provided my political greening. I didn't want grades and I did want to voice my opinion." He and several other students from his department conducted a survey, and even though the results of that study were inconclusive, they presented them to the committee responsible for considering the grade change issue. "I learned how to separate individuals and issues and to work within the system for change. I learned how to work with people."

If your own values are crystallized, you can develop short- and long-term goals, decide where you fit in best.

Clubs, and there are hundreds of them on some campuses, give you an opportunity to develop leadership roles and meet people. If you join a business students' club, for example, you will get to know what the job market is like. You can also begin to make contacts for the future by bringing influential people to visit and speak on your campus. In considering a club, ask yourself what you can expect from it and what you can give to it.

As a returning student, consider a project with a clearly defined beginning and end point. This may be far more manageable than an ongoing club or committee. Here are some limited projects students have reported as ways to attain recognition.

- In a university that had no literary magazine, a student collected works by faculty, students, and alumni and produced a single edition. This brought her into close contact with the faculty and administration. It also helped her revise her career choice; she decided *not* to enter academia as planned.
- A student worked as a student assistant to a psychology professor and did biofeedback research with insomniac patients. He became very involved with the members of the psychology department.
- In a college that offered no reentry program for students, an undergraduate requested permission and some funds to inquire at other institutions and came up with a plan. This brought her in contact with the administration. Later she was offered a position as coordinator for the reentry program at another institution.

We remember a beautiful young student who was asked

by her history professor to act as a student assistant for a course he taught one summer. As an older reentry woman watched her, she thought to herself, "I could do that." Her feelings prompted her to apply for a small grant, which enabled her to teach an experimental course in communications.

Grants, incidentally, are an excellent way to seek out avenues for your existing talents or to develop unknown ones. Grants are big business, and colleges often maintain full-time staffs to try to obtain them. Investigate projects and small research grants. Furthermore, find out which professors have grants for large projects. Ask to research, write, or even type for them. Ask teachers for names of their associations' trade magazines and newletters. Read them for additional ideas.

Another way through the stone walls of your institution is to get a job on campus. There is more to this than working for the money. Library assistants, recreation assistants, tutors, paper graders, and campus bus drivers all have a special vantage point in the organization.

You don't have to be a graduate student or wait to be asked to participate in these special experiences. Go back to school with the positive attitude that you expect people to be open and flexible to your needs. Confront your adviser. Say, "I want to do something special."

No one has the investment in your future that you do. Do one great—at least great for you—activity outside your regular class work. You won't regret it.

15

Friends and Lovers

Although you may feel lonely when you return to a campus of your choice, you *can* make friends if you wish to. Your first inclination may be to choose people of your age and background. Stifle this urge, or at least look for friendships in other age brackets or cultures at a later date when you feel more secure. Younger people don't feel the same barrier about age when they share a common experience. Furthermore, this may be the only time in your life when you will have a chance to be with people from other cultures.

When Frances, the mother of three high school students, returned to college for a business degree, two young women approached her after a class one evening and asked if she would like to form a study group with them. She wasn't sure how she would fit in. "I was almost old enough to be their mother," she recalls. "Would we be able to relate to each other? They both seemed so bright. My worries were completely unfounded. Now we study for all major exams together and go out after class for a cup of coffee."

One of us had the opportunity to make friends with another returning student who was black. Traveling from the inner city, she took two buses and a train round-trip each day from her apartment in a heavily demolished urban area. She was intelligent, regal, and on the same wavelength as we were. It was a pleasure and a treat to know her.

Minority students have echoed the same sentiment. John J., who is now a computer operator, says, "I was lovingly broadened through racial contact. My new insights were translated into how I live on a daily basis."

OLD FRIENDSHIPS

New school friendships often disrupt the old ones—for better or worse. Old friends may not be very pleased about your making new ones and view it as a reflection of your future relationship with them. Or they may feel threatened by the new knowledge you are gaining in school. Your vocabulary changes as a matter of course, and the idiom of your work seeps into your conversation—you now use words like *idiom* while you may not have before. You may also find that your old friends no longer interest you as they did before.

In making a new commitment of time, effort, and emotional outlay, stop and think how you wish to handle old friendships. We found that saying to good friends, "I am busy now. Please put me on hold," worked well. Most of our good friends respected our needs. One of us even had an old friend who kept us posted on up-to-date news of people and activities in the "real world." Old friends are a comfortable known quantity. Your common "remember when" history provides a zone of stability.

Yet the opportunity to explore new friendships is one of the unsung benefits of returning to school. New friends can help you develop your new self. For example, our collaboration on this book is a direct result of a friendship made between returning students.

FINDING NEW FRIENDS

A friend can mean a lot of different things to different

people. One type of friend may say, "I care about you and what you are doing," and another might become a social friend as well by entering into your lifestyle of activities. Reentry students seem to encounter fewer of the latter. In the renaissance of adult education, part-time study has increased in popularity; study, parenting, and jobs impinge on time for socializing. Even college-age students attending school full-time have joined the work force. At the University of Iowa, 70 percent of the students work. At urban commuter colleges students "stop-out" for whole semesters and return again.

You must be willing to take the initiative and give people more than one chance. If they don't meet you halfway, it doesn't necessarily mean they dislike you. They may not be open to getting to know you because of the time factor. A lot depends upon what students' priorities are.

Remember, too, that the spontaneity essential to friendship is destroyed when the focus is on keeping score of who does what for whom. Some tips for making new friendships in school follow:

1. Join a club or organization.
2. Say "Yes" to a group invitation such as, "Anyone for coffee?"
3. Make the first move.
4. Do a favor for someone.
5. Ask someone for help.

As Leefeldt and Callenbach note in their book, *The Art of Friendship*, "We have observed that the single most important strategy for finding new friends is to concentrate on your own real interests which open new possibilities for relating to new people. Nothing makes you so attractive as being engrossed in some activity that truly engages your talents and intelligence."

YOUR IMAGE

When we returned to school, we were concerned about

our age and how it would affect our relationship with younger students and with professors. Some older students went to great lengths to dress "young," which meant jeans and the right length of sideburns for men, the natural look for women. Our great fear was that we would be mistaken for someone's mother. And we were! The experience of the years was written not only in the fine lines of our faces, but in the work we did in class. Young students were shocked, sometimes intimidated by our conscientious behavior; we were equally shocked by their lack of class participation and their late homework assignments.

Yet our worries about age and acceptance were generally unfounded. We were appreciated by our teachers, too, who welcomed students who were sincerely interested in being in the classroom. Some of the women even wore skirts again!

FRIENDSHIPS WITH FACULTY

Can students and professors be friends?

"I became friends with a lot of mine," says a Vietnam veteran. "We went out and drank beer together. It has a lot to do with mutual interests and age."

"No," says the dean of continuing education in a Detroit-based university. "Not social friends. I've gone golfing with some of my students; I don't include them at a cocktail party at my house."

A woman, now a teacher herself, says she had a terrific friendship with an older female teacher. They would dine out together or even go out together with their dates. "She helped me develop into a strong woman while acting as a role model, but I suppose it was partly a mentor relationship for me then. Now that I am employed and have credentials, our friendship seems more equal."

Other students have held out the glove of friendship and watched it flutter to the ground. "I've tried on occasion to become friends with professors," says one student, "and it has not worked, so I just dropped the idea for the future."

Obviously, reentry students, who might at first glance appear to be likely candidates for social friends among faculty, have had a wide range of experiences. Remember that colleges are bureaucracies and small towns. The people in them operate the way the rest of the business world does—in this case, fighting for grants, tenure, and contacts with the right people. And highly skilled and educated people prefer being with their own peer group. Friendships are often based on the answers to questions they ask themselves: "What do you have to offer? What do I have to give?"

A few teachers do reach out for friendships among students and are quite ready to welcome them. A teacher in the business school of one university says, "I just came back from a meeting with several student representatives. It took them all weekend to loosen up and finally call me by my first name. When I go out to consult in industry and see former students now in positions of rank, they invariably continue calling me Doctor. I wish they would stop this nonsense. It sets up a barrier, which I don't like. I wish students would come forward in friendship."

We knew a reentry student in a theater arts program who brought the new dean of her department into her established circle of theater friends. Not only did they become friends, but upon completing her degree she was appointed to work with the children's theater, then later appointed to the faculty.

If becoming friendly with professors and administrators feels comfortable to you, why not pursue it? The option is certainly yours. Dale Carnegie's book, *How to Win Friends and Influence People,* with its ninety-five printings and almost eight million copies sold, is a testament to people's continued search for friendship. There is no reason why the search should not continue on campus.

LOVERS

In the play *Pygmalion,* by George Bernard Shaw, Colonel

Pickering asks his friend, Professor Higgins, about his feelings toward student Eliza Doolittle, whom he has just salvaged from a Covent Garden vegetable market. The professor answers that the relationship between student and teacher is "sacred."

One real-life professor laughed at this idea, adding, "Boys will be boys and girls will lead them on." A counselor at a community college adds further, "And girls will be girls and boys will lead them on!" A reentry male had recently been in her office to complain about being sexually harassed by his female teacher.

Despite Professor Higgins's moralistic tone, the fact is, sex between students and professors is a fact of campus life. And while braless, nubile eighteen- to twenty-two-year-olds may seem especially appealing, the possibilities for sexual alliances among all ages and combinations of genders are likely in our highly permissive and sexually charged society. As Larry Rochell stated in his article, "Sex Roles on Campus: Does Professor Charles Really Get His Angels?" in *Community College Frontiers,* "Many professors have reached a point in their lives when they are ready for something new. . . . Nearing 40, dissertations in hand, tenure track begun, male instructors are ready for anything. Slight flirtations are begun in class; favorite female students receive smiles, pats on shoulders, invitations to the offices, invitations to lunch. And then what?"

Because of the new tone of campuses, with courses and teaching methods more personally oriented, the classical Christmas party given by the professor may be giving way to the friendly lunch. And the divorcee, the midlife crisis matron or male who has come to school with a commitment to make a new and better life, may also include lunch on their lists.

"But professors are so boring," says one thirty-three-year-old, twice-divorced reentry student. "They arc just like doctors; they're narrow specialists. I haven't met one yet I'd like to know better." Aside from this disclaimer, women *are* intrigued by male professors. When *Glamour* magazine ran a campus report in a 1980 issue asking which factors figured most prominently in women's attraction to professors, most of the women cited, in order, (1) "good rapport or friendship," (2) "his intellect," and (3) "sexual attraction."

Dr. Maj-Britt Rosenbaum, associate clinical professor of psychiatry at Albert Einstein Medical College in New York, was asked to comment. She believed these women were denying the unconscious aspects. "The teacher in the class for that moment is the dominant male in the group, and in many mammalian groups, that is the most sexually active and erotic male. Intellect," she continued, "is a sexualized male attribute in this culture—it makes him more male, sexier, more attractive. It's the opposite of the dumb blonde."

But what finally intrigues the majority of women, especially when the teacher is older, appears to be his authority position. The fact that he may be unreachable makes him even more desirable.

Or, as an attractive older male literature professor states bluntly, "A woman returning to school doesn't want to go home again to that clod of a husband—the salesman, accountant, or professional. She wants to hang around school and talk to her literature professor!"

What happens next in this not-so-unusual college soap opera. Will our heroine live secretly with her fantasies and stay true to the "clod"? Or will she acquire a built-in library when our hypothetical professor *tosses over* mortgage, kids, wife, and 900-page book-in-process? Tune in next year when fantasies have either vanished into smoke—or they are nicely ensconced in a two bedroom flat five miles from town.

"I see nothing wrong with two grown people getting together in any way they wish," says a student who had an affair with her psychology teacher that lasted two years. "He was very sophisticated and helped me with my career." On further questioning, she added, "He dropped me for another student. I felt wounded; I got over him eventually and now look back at the experience as one that helped me develop as a woman."

Professors agree that the opportunities exist. Students and teachers have affairs and even get married, but as a rule, teachers are careful to avoid sexual relationships, especially with undergraduates. "When there is a young coed who finds me attractive, I thank her for the compliment and tell her I will have to wait until she graduates because I never play where I work. Now sometimes that's not easy to do," says one professor at a large university.

Both teachers and students seem to agree that the student is in the inferior power position and thus may lose more than the teacher. But suppose a student does not wish to reciprocate the professor's interest. How can he or she best handle the situation to protect class standing and salvage a teacher/student relationship without feeling the course must be dropped? One thirty-five-year-old student handled it this way: "Because I have been out in the business world, I think I know how to handle unwanted advances pretty well. The trick is to make a nice joke of it without laughing. I treat the requester as one who has done no harm in asking. Be gratified that they found you appealing, because they must have. I'm never insulted."

Now that more and more women are appearing on faculties, similar situations are beginning to occur with males in the inferior power position. A returning male student complained about specific advances from a female instructor. He said he felt in charge but wanted to let the counselor know about it. "The best way to handle that," says the counselor, "is to let the administration take care of it. I may not believe it's true, but I will confront the instructor and say, 'A student said this about you.'"

There are laws against the harassment of women. Affirmative action makes a lot of noise about it and women are not afraid to come forward. That is the first impediment for professors pursuing sexual favors. The likelihood of conflict arising in existing relationships is very high, which is another hazard. Finally, as one woman relates, "You have to be superdiscreet. You cannot tell your friends you are sleeping with your professor or they will despise you for unfairly raising the class curve."

PART IV:
FACING PROBLEMS

16

Anxiety

Returning students have every right to be anxious. Making a commitment to change your life, hopefully for the better, is frightening. Although some people appear to absorb stress without showing emotional or behavioral distress, few individuals actually manage to avoid anxiety altogether.

Among others are the A student who says, "I am terrified every time I take an exam," the returning student who has a secret terror of failing to get a degree, and the person who says, "I am afraid that people will see me as too old and funny-looking to be a student." Each returning student has his or her own area of stress. Other pressures may include personal variables such as job responsibilities, family obligations, and guilt about neglect of children or spouse.

Each person also solves these problems differently, depending on previous background. It would be impossible to construct a set of rules or answers applicable to each reentry student's problem. However, by understanding stress agents, identifying them in your own school experience, and finding some coping skills to manage them, you can maintain good physical and mental well-being.

GRADES

So your palms are sweaty and your rash is back! It must be exam time.

No matter how many times profs say, "Just relax and enjoy learning," no matter how clever and witty they are in front of the class, they still give tests to see what you have gleaned from their witty remarks and the assigned text. Returning students report that grades are a great source of anxiety.

"Grades *are* a terrible source of pressure," says one community college instructor who teaches composition. "It is hard to go back to school. You want to say something to the teacher to show her what you know. You are not dumb! But what you're afraid of is that you *are* dumb. After the first exam the pressure lessens."

The same instructor, who was once a returning student herself, has great empathy for her students. "If you stick with me," she tells them, "you'll make it even if I have to pull you through by the hair. And if you work hard, you have an excellent chance to get a B. I never fail students if they do the work." You cannot count on every prof being as supportive, though by and large they *do* want you to succeed. Meanwhile, we unfairly tend to equate academic success with personal worth: if you receive an A you are a good person; if you receive a failing grade, you are a bad person. This is certainly not true.

PEOPLE PROBLEMS

If you could sit at home and take instruction from a professor on a television screen and avoid interacting with anything except the TV screen, your stress might be diminished. For years, advocates of widespread educational use of our various media have claimed that university buildings would no longer be necessary if students learned at home with the television screen as their classroom. This, of course, is preposterous, as any returning student can tell you, for while people are a source of stress in your day-to-day communications, they are also our source of inspiration.

Nevertheless, confronted by an administration and faculty in a bureaucratic setting, anxiety-laden situations can be formidable. A loss of transcript or mislaid papers can take weeks to straighten out. A disagreement with a professor can give you a sleepless night. A computer that says you haven't returned a book, when you know full well you have (unless your son has thrown it under his bed with his football helmet), can make a foe of your friendly librarian.

One student reports, "I came back to school prepared and confident to enter graduate school after a former teaching career that ended fifteen years before. It was a total shock to me to find that I couldn't analyze the material in my literature class as well as my professor expected. Furthermore, she was a young female professor, and I had the feeling she was equating me with her mother! The stress I felt was enormous."

Now listen to the thoughts of two different professors: "Students put us up on a pedestal. They think because we have a Ph.D. we know everything, and consequently they are as scared as hell and are afraid even to speak up in class," said one. The other professor adds, "I have taught for twenty-five years. I am in the classroom because *I* know more about the subject than the students do. *I'll* control the conversation!"

No wonder new students are anxious before they learn to psyche out the prof. What does he or she expect of you? Are you going to make it?

MAKING IT

The bottom line is success. Older women and retired men returning to school for enrichment might be thought to be less anxious because job security is not their goal, yet they are eager to prove to themselves and to their families that they are still good learners. Women who have divested themselves of volunteer work and bridge games under the impetus of the liberated '70s are eager to be successful, whatever that may mean to them. We have seen casually dressed matrons in designer jeans laboring endless hours over a paper or project in their personal quest for excellence.

Those who are returning to college and are unemployed or updating their credentials may feel a particular strain. Imagine the pressure on the returnee who has for years been a computer programmer at a large steel company and is the only one in his corporation department without a degree. Or the anxiety of a plant manager who, instead of going to repeated seminars, asks to go back to school and get a degree. Both are being financed by their employers.

"Not only do my wife and kids keep an eye on my progress," says one, "but my boss does, too. I don't dare be a failure."

Arching like an umbrella over these school-related causes of anxiety are the general societal stresses we all feel. People are more mobile and family ties are looser than in the past. Returning students are in an age bracket in which loss of a spouse or parent may create havoc in their lives. Changes occur so rapidly that, voluntary or forced, pleasant or unpleasant, they all require adjustment.

RECOGNIZING ANXIETY

While driving around precipitous curves on a mountainside without side rails, your fear may be great. But once you arrive at your destination, you feel a sense of relief—your fear is over; it is finite. It is only when the frightening stimulus has no end that you feel long-term stress. When that occurs, body-mind illnesses such as high blood pressure and disorders of the digestive system begin. They frequently happen without warning, before you are even aware of their onslaught.

You should be able to recognize undue stress through its symptoms: insomnia, lack of concentration, faulty short-term memory, and a jittery feeling. There is no question that undue stress affects our thoughts, feelings, and our bodies.

STRATEGIES FOR COMBATING STRESS

First of all, remember that everyone feels stress. Returning students tend to view other successful people among the students, faculty, and administration as achieving goals with minimal effort, great self-confidence, few errors, and little stress. The unflattering picture they present of themselves is simply false.

We met one apparent paradigm of perfection in a class during the '70s. Now working in the urban planning field, Bill was a great A student who exuded self-confidence. When asked whether he had ever felt any anxiety as a returning student, he blinked his eyes unbelievingly and answered, "Me? My God, I ran so scared that I studied twice as much as anyone else."

We recently sat in on a university planning committee and listened to faculty members and administrators voice opposing and sometimes angry views. Although they kept the decibel level low, they put out enough adrenalin to float the conference room onto the football field.

The point here is that you must avoid such distorted thinking about other people and focus on your own competencies.

Next, leave your mistakes behind you. If you receive a poor grade, determine what you did wrong and then forget about the grade. We learn through our failures as well as our successes. Dwelling on past errors takes valuable energy that can be diverted to constructive action. A study done at Pennsylvania State University by Michael Mahoney and his collaborators showed that male gymnasts who qualified for Olympic competition thought less of past failures than did those who failed to qualify.

Learn to make a friend of failure. Take him out to lunch, ask him what went wrong, then tell him you have a heavy schedule and won't be able to see him for a long time.

Learn to differentiate the stressful situations that can be changed (1) easily, (2) somewhat, or (3) not at all. You can easily receive course counseling if that is your source of stress; you can drop a course before the drop/add period, but you might need to consider its consequences in terms of your degree requirement and delay or postpone your objective; you cannot get credit for a course unless you do the work!

In other words, don't beat your head against a stone wall. It may take time to analyze each stress, as above, but when you do, you will be able to act accordingly. And deciding on a plan of action is the first step toward relieving stress.

SPECIFIC STRATEGIES TO HELP FILTER STRESS

1. *Find a support group among friends, family, or school counselors.* They can help you solve problems. Colleges, especially those oriented toward reentry students, have programs or courses to make your transition easier. A side benefit of this is making contact with others at an early stage.

2. *At the same time as you seek support, take the responsibility for getting things done.* You are your own best friend. If you habitually bite off more than you can chew, thereby programming yourself for failure, you should aim for reducing your load. If you are a married, unemployed woman whose husband is unable or not eager to advance your tuition, inquire about available financial aid on your own.

3. *Clarify your values.* Actually sit down and think about them. Having a framework or philosophy to work from can lessen the stress of decision making.

4. *Do not push yourself beyond your endurance.* Alternate intense effort with recreation or reduced work. All schools have sport facilities. Plan on arriving forty-five minutes before class to swim or jog.

5. *Avoid insisting on perfection in yourself and others.* If

you have half a cup, it is half full, not half empty. Learn patience and tolerance by putting yourself in the other fellow's place. Is that cranky older prof worried about his waning powers? Is that prof who is younger than you worried about his or her ability to live up to *your* real-life experiences?

6. *Build personal esteem and accomplishments one step at a time.* Great successes are built on countless little ones. Success in one professor's course might lead him to ask you to work on his research project, which might in turn lead you to employment, which might in fact lead you eventually to the top of the corporation. Don't believe that those rags-to-riches stories are accomplished in one easy leap. With rare exceptions, successful people have paved their own way to the top; sometimes they just "forget" how long it took them to get there. A good example is the stories we have all read about "new" authors who supposedly became best-selling writers without any prior experience, when in fact they have been participating in writing workshops for years or preparing speeches for delivery in their banks or corporations.

7. *Find a personal stability zone.* We know a psychiatrist who savors fine wines. He has placed an easy chair, a lamp, and books in his wine cellar, where he keeps his wine racks. He relaxes there, experiencing the bouquet of the wines. Students have told us they always wear a certain sweater or shirt on an exam day; others find stability in music, meditation, or a shopping trip.

Finally, remember that everyone becomes accustomed to new situations. That is why you are able to take on larger and larger loads of schoolwork. Just as runners condition their bodies and run faster and farther, your capabilities will increase. Time is on your side.

17

Special Problems of Male Returning Students

When prospective male students consider enrolling in an institution of higher education, they are more concerned with improving their practical skills than any other factor. As some companies begin to change their technology, and men are becoming technologically unemployable, the need for a new career or a career with a new emphasis may become a necessity.

Men's career changes are generally mid-life changes that occur somewhere between the ages of thirty-five and fifty. At this age, men and women share several common problems upon returning to school. For instance, both feel the pressure of time: How do you go back to school, juggle work, and take care of your family? Lack of time can affect the temperament and outlook of both male and female returning students. Yet men have a decided edge over women in several areas.

Men receive more outside incentives from their employers. Industry spends millions of dollars a year picking up the tab for employees. Wives often work for the special reason of helping to put their husbands through school.

Further help comes from the G.I. Bill, which has been a boon to male returning students, and well they deserve it. G.I. benefits offer $450 a month to a married man with one child. They also include an allowance of up to $850 for private tutoring during the student's college career. (For more information on veterans' benefits, see Part II, Chapter 10.)

Dealing with authority seems to be a less serious problem for men than for women. At work they have been trained to be task-oriented, to focus on what the job is, how it can be done best, and who the best person is to carry it through. The spirit of team play, which they learned as boys, is the focus of their style.

Men also seem to be better prepared in math and sciences. Until recently, these subjects were assumed to be more appropriate for male learners as the basis for their future work in the trades and professions.

Because men who are returning to school have been out there slugging it out in the "real world," they are also aware of how the system works. "The higher a man's office and title, the less you know what he does," is only one of many observations men make about the nature of the working place. "When I begin a new job," says another, "I keep a very low profile until I find out who really has clout in the organization, who I have to watch, and who can be my friend." Women are just beginning to learn about office politics.

All this adds up to a more assertive human being who can deal better with the realities of the marketplace. And while all men are not equally adept in these skills, until very recent times they have had the cutting edge.

Finally, the male student may have to modify his lifestyle far less than the returning woman student. Studies support the notion that women, whether working or in school, still maintain the responsibility for children, household chores, social engagements, and the family meals. Men concern themselves mainly with work and school. And although the demands of both are extremely pressing, men can usually focus their attention in two areas rather than ten.

It would be a mistake, however, to paint an overly rosy picture of men's reentry into higher education. Men with the optimum financial backing, family support, and confidence have difficulties. Some are caused by lack of experience; others are of a more psychological nature.

THE MAN IN THE ARMORED SUIT

For a long time women repressed their feelings. Only with the advent of the women's movement and the increasing number of women with careers did they begin talking more openly among themselves. While women's rap groups have grown dramatically on campuses, personal growth classes offered to men at colleges and universities have drawn little participation. Men appear to dislike courses in which they have to express their feelings.

Men have always been less encouraged by societal structures to be open. "In the corporate structures, you perform a job assigned to you and keep your feelings bottled up," says a returning male student. "Men aren't supposed to complain or cry."

One woman shared an anecdote about her student husband. "I have never heard him cry," she reports. "But last month when we went away for a weekend at a nearby resort to relax, I gave him *A Christmas Story,* by Truman Capote. He took it into the next room to read it. Suddenly I heard these sobs. I ran in to see what was wrong, fearing a total disaster. He was sobbing because of the story. He was so embarrassed."

The armored suit, taken off on occasion, doesn't, however, extend its protection to feelings about women.

CONFUSED RELATIONSHIPS

Women's liberation has left some men perplexed about their relationship with women. It goes far beyond the simplicities of opening a door for a woman or paying for her meal. For men, particularly those over thirty-five, who have not developed insights and clarification of the new values of women's roles, this perplexity may border on outright rage.

"Men are quite frankly frightened by the assertive woman," says one university counselor who works with male groups in his private practice. " 'Well, that one is just a bitch,' a man might complain. That same man oftentimes avoids female professors. When this happens, I want to know what kind of female experience the man has had and how it has related to his feelings about women. If he has a docile wife, there is probably a reason he chose her, and probably a reason he is afraid to deal with assertive women. If he can learn some honest communication skills— 'I feel very put out at your assertiveness,' 'I feel such-and-such a way,'—it would help him immensely to cope with the assertive woman."

As one male student notes, adding to his general confusion about the "new" woman, "I find that female professors have women working exclusively on their research projects while male teachers have both men and women. They (women) are fighting to get in, and when they do they keep you out."

Younger male students seem more able to handle the competition and attitudes of the "new" woman. They grew up with her in the '60s. As one says, "You make your own breaks. People who are confident feel this way. You don't blame aggressive women or minorities for your not getting the breaks."

Well, at least men have a good buddy system and friends. Right? Not so, say the experts. Because of all the publicity about male networks in the business world, we tend to equate this with meaningful friendships, which is certainly a different thing.

Most men, in fact, have not had close personal friends since high school or former college days. While women are capable of experiencing real intimacy with other women and have supporting friendships, men are less able to do so. Our particular culture, in addition to teaching us that men don't cry, teaches us that men don't touch (with the exception of a handshake). This, of course, would be unthinkable in many other nations, where kisses and hugs among members of the same sex are the norm.

"There seems to remain an undisclosed fear that intimacy is somehow linked to sexuality and, therefore, the homosexual relationship," says one school psychologist. "Consequently, many men may have drinking buddies, but their relationship remains superficial and nontrusting."

COMPETITION

Men returning to school often fear competing with young students; they are afraid that their younger classmates will run circles around them in tests. Or they feel they must compete with the good student, who, perhaps for a variety of reasons, has a great deal of time to study. A grade of C means average, and men don't like that word. Male students, often from blue-collar occupations, are embarrassed to take time off from work, and therefore may take ten years to complete school, taking one course at a time.

Overriding all the previous items, and the biggest stumbling block for returning male students, is money. If they are the breadwinners in the family, they feel morally obliged to do their share. For some, college means dependency on others, which can be an uncomfortable feeling. Pride and habit keep people routed in the same tracks, but if you feel ready to put your foot into the waters of change, you might want to consider the following tips.

1. Find a peer group at college to stimulate new friendships and exchanges of ideas. If you wish to formalize it with a leader, ask a male counselor from the counseling office or psychology department to lead the group. If you are a veteran, you might want to do it through the college's veterans' affairs office.

2. Find a mentor who will help you with your new set of

goals. In one school, the instructor in class was invited to speak at a student's plant. From that invitation, a friendly bond developed.

3. Take the time to discuss your feelings as the occasions occur. Maybe your partner or teacher can offer ideas or be a sounding board. Continually bottled up feelings are what heart attacks are made of.

4. Try to be more understanding of that woman who seems overly assertive to you. Remember, women haven't been asserting themselves openly for very long.

5. If you are not trying to get into a highly competitive graduate school, such as medicine or law, try not to think of grades as life-and-death matters. When you take the pressure off yourself and let the course work come to you in a relaxed enjoyable way, you often improve your performance. Alternate tough courses with less difficult ones.

Finally, if financial pressure becomes too great, "stop out" for a semester to catch your breath and catch up on cash. Before you do this, however, check out financial aid in your school.

Our society puts tremendous pressure on men to be successful and to achieve. Even though your return to school indicates that you are goal-oriented, at times you must say to society and its demands, "I'll do it my way."

THREE RETURNING MALE STUDENTS SPEAK UP

Name: John L.
Age: 29
Major: Labor Studies
Home: West Virginia

"I was raised with five brothers and sisters in a union family. My father, grandfather, and uncles worked in the mines. Workers were always around my home. My uncle died in an accident in the mines, and my grandfather died of black lung disease.

"During my first college experience, I attended school on a football scholarship and studied art. I quit school because it was dull and enlisted in the Marines for three years where I served as a military policeman. Basically, what I've learned since I've been out of school is that it's not what you know, but who you know.

"After I got out of the service, I worked as a millwright and machinist in a steel mill. My wife's father is president of a major steel worker's union. I got involved in the union, too, and had a chance to take a test for a position as arbitrator with the state industrial commission. I didn't get the job (even though I passed the test) because the other applicants had either more experience or more education. That made me think! I decided to go back to school. Only a handful of people have a degree in labor studies. My degree should help me become an officer or steward of a local union.

"Although I was an average student the first time around, I'm in the honor society now with a 3.5 grade average. I try to maintain As. The whole thing is sort of political. It is really not learning-oriented. I don't think you work for the grades. You have to know how to get them.

"In order to improve a grade, a B for example, I go crying to the instructor. Of course, you have to be able to react to the kind of instructor, to know his personality.

"Being noticed in class gives you a plus. In the first part of the term, I express a lot of interest, make a lot of comments. That way my name is always the first one to be learned by the instructor. That's my number one goal. When they start sleeping on me, I'm not afraid to let them know I am there, nor am I afraid to debate. I don't like to point out when they are wrong publicly, but later I'll go up to them. They appreciate that you didn't point it out in class. Most of my corrections are based more on my background and general life experience. You have to remember I lived with the unions. I point out where the book is wrong.

"A lot of your grade comes from class interaction. It has been necessary to drop some classes, especially in the business field, where instructors think I'm a radical because I'm studying labor relations. I drop a course before I'm penalized and take it another time.

"I ask around about who the good instructors are and

who is more liberal with his grades, especially if it is a hard course. I even ask other instructors for that information. They will tell you. Many of the instructors around here are my age, so we can relate to each other. You have to express interest in what *they* are doing in order to come across.

"I avoid part-time teachers who have other work outside, particularly in the junior college setting. I had a midterm in business law to make up because of illness. I left messages and must have gone over a dozen times to this lawyer's office to find him. Another part-time teacher I had was a very poor instructor. After three sessions, all the students were asleep. He had used up all his material. I questioned him about the plant where he was employed during the day, and I tried to keep things alive in the classroom. I think that it is best to be a full-time day student whenever possible because during the day (at this school) you have more full-time teachers.

"I measure my own worth by myself. I know that I am no dummy, and I don't allow anyone to think I am one. The disadvantage of being an outspoken student is that it is easy to turn the class against you. I try to be persuasive about the disadvantages and advantages of being my kind of person and about the things I believe. I admit my biggest problem in my return to school has been learning to keep my mouth shut. I get upset with these younger kids coming to school. They have so adapted to the system. They sit and listen to teacher and don't say anything.

"If I am very involved in a course, I'll read the material several times and feel well prepared for the exam. If I don't particularly care for the course, I find someone in class who does have an interest and has taken good notes. Before exams, I'll ask him if I can go over his notes with him. It helps both of us. A lot of people are willing to do that.

"Where there are a large number of dates and names and memory work, the only way to get ready for an exam is to cram and hit it from all angles. There is no way to retain all this. My major memory strategy is the use of association.

For example, in my history of photography course, a fellow by the name of Nader went up in a balloon, which was basically unsafe to do, and took large panoramic pictures. I made the association with Ralph Nader, who wouldn't approve of an unsafe vehicle.

"As far as my grades go, the first thing I do early in the course is to ask the instructor, 'How do I get an A? I want an A, I'll settle for a B, but I don't want anything lower than that.' If we have a test and I do poorly—get a C or even a D—I go up to the instructor and ask what I can do to raise the grade. 'Can I bring in some extra work?' It is important that you express that desire.

"Generally, I am a good test taker. I play the percentages; I'm a gambler. If I can narrow multiple-choice questions to two, I'll answer the question. In an essay test, you have to write down as much as relates to the subject. The volume counts. Before I answer the test question, I read the instructions very carefully. 'What is the most important use of photography in this country today?' was one of my test questions. All the answers seemed correct. Knowing the system, that always means the *best* answer, I chose only one of them. As it turned out, they were all right. I felt kind of deceived. It is not going to hurt me that much. It is one of the instructors to whom I always bring a cup of coffee. That helps, too.

"In class I usually try to sit in the outside row, second row from the front. I don't sit in the front row so as not to appear too eager. Very few people sit in the front row. I can still get attention from the instructor since there is no one in the first row. I can see the whole class that way, too, because there is no one on the other side of me. I learn just as much from the students as I do from the teacher.

"I am a very competitive person. I don't know if it is good or bad. The grading system is highly competitive. I don't think there should be any failures unless someone is totally disinterested. People have had small failures in their lives, and they never forget them. But we shouldn't eliminate competition either because that is what our country is based on, and it is out there in real life. The new teachers are into a more human way of grading and planning. The major problem in the educational system is that they don't teach you how to learn; they tell you what to learn.

"I read a lot of books on how to improve myself and how to beat the system. Two of my favorites are *How to Get Control of Your Time and Your Life,* by Alan Lakein, and *How to Win Friends and Influence People,* by Dale Carnegie. I have also studied Abraham Maslow's work in my courses, *Industrial Organizations in Society* and *Human Relations.*

"The Marines have taught me a lot of self-discipline and survivability. I can survive any situation; no matter what happens, I can get through and be on top of it.

"What I feel best about school now is that it is not in vain. I am not just going through college this time and taking up space."

Name: Werner W.
Age: 38
Major: Business
Home: Michigan

"I am a tool-and-die worker, the father of three, two of them teenagers. I have been going to college at night for five years, taking one or two courses each semester. Two years before I started school, I was made a supervisor and only lasted five months because I didn't have the skills.

"I study Sunday morning when everyone is asleep. When I have a lot to do, I get up at 4:00 A.M. and study for a couple of hours before I go to work at 7:00. I am anxious about grades before every exam.

"You have to know what teachers want. It takes about four weeks to find out what kind of questions they are going to ask, whether they are mostly from the text or lectures. A good teacher is someone who doesn't teach over the level of the student's head.

"I sit right up front during class time. It is less distracting; you don't see other students. I am a B student. I can pick out a few students who are going to be smarter than anyone else in the class, almost from the first day. I don't let it bother me. I learn from them.

"I get a lot of encouragement from home. Mostly, my wife pushes me when I slack off. I got an A in my first course, and it gave me a good boost. My children are better students now than before the time I started back to school. We compare grades and cheer each other on."

Name: Ed J.
Age: 43
Major: Social Science
Home: Pennsylvania

"I was passive in class at first. But as I became more confident, I found the professors really appreciated the insights I gained and practical experience I had received in my work as a policeman.

"At a small college like Bucks, I never felt that the instructors or professors felt threatened by my maturity and experience. But at Temple, it was different. Because of the size of the classes, I found the professors to be more numbers-oriented than human-oriented. However, because my field was sociology and psychology, it was more acceptable to relate personal experiences to the material. My experience as a policeman and as a family man were important because I could relate more personally to the problems and theories we discussed.

"My study habits were a bit unconventional. They had to be. Holding down three jobs was quite a trick. There were no large blocks of time available. However, as a mature student, I think I looked for more; I was concerned about how I could apply what I learned to the present and the future. And I was determined to make a better life for my family."

18

Some Special Problems for Women

Annette J. was the pillar of the community; she toured with her children's class on endless field trips and had milk and brownies ready for them at three o'clock. If she had had her choice, she never would have stopped being a mother and homemaker. Then one day her husband told her he was leaving her to make a new life. For Annette, a reentry to school was a harsh decision made in the wake of a marriage gone bad.

"I guess I'm sort of the classic case," says Annette. "When you're past forty, it is difficult retooling yourself. Sometimes I got very down. I had lost all my youthful confidence when I returned to the outside world."

Divorced women comprise a large segment of women returning to school. Their reentry can be as traumatic as a spacecraft's splashdown. Their difficult situation is frequently complicated by lack of funds, lack of family support, and the need to find adequate child care for their children. At the same time, they must also deal with the loss of self-confidence that often follows divorce.

For women in Annette's position, school provides a

wonderful comfort zone. *Here they are surrounded by people who are receptive to change.* Annette's first task should be to find a support group within her school, either one for reentry students or one for single parents. She will find other women in the same set of circumstances. Spending time discussing the kinds of conflicts they are experiencing can speed her toward readjustment.

However, in any situation of readjustment, allowing enough time for a transition is essential. "Don't expect overnight miracles," says one newly divorced returning student. "Tell yourself you are doing a little better today than yesterday, and put your yesterdays behind you."

Margaret S. is pretty and lively. She was what some people call an overachiever; she paced herself with one course each semester and did magnificiently. Because she returned to school without definite goals, she was thought by some students and professors to be a dilettante.

In her eagerness, Margaret's problem was that she had never learned what younger students understand as the rules of classroom behavior: a student doesn't run on with personal experiences, ask incessant questions, monopolize class time, continually corner the instructor for private conversations, or write a fifteen-page paper when the assignment calls for four!

In the world from which Margaret came—doing good works for philanthropic organizations and attending lecture programs—her kind of input and enthusiasm was valued. Even in the college setting a few teachers, though they would never acknowledge it, looked to her to revive their sometimes dying class session.

Margaret needn't make any excuses for her outstanding record of straight As. The fact that she was toting up credits to get a degree for a purpose that seemed unknown is really her concern. As she candidly states, "I will never have to work, and I have no definite career plans, but I love school and the stimulation of a classroom." The sheer joy of learning is reason enough to attend college, but what about Margaret's classroom behavior?

It often takes us years to see that the way we are doing
something may need changing. There is something to be
learned in taking criticism, and how we handle it determines how we change and grow. Margaret believed students were jealous of her. It took her several semesters of
school and a talk with a sympathetic counselor to begin to
modify her classroom behavior without compromising the
high standards she set for herself.

Joanne L. is a young minority woman, the first of her
family to attend college. She has two little girls, Dawn and
Davida. Her husband, Al, who drives a taxi, was not happy
to hear Joanne say she wanted to go to college. He wanted
her to stay home with the children and get a part-time job.
Joanne persisted in her big dream and finally wore Al
down; she enrolled in a local college with high hopes and
her husband's grudging consent.

"Before school, I get up and dress my kids and take them
to a day care center," says Joanne. "Then I take the bus to
school and try to get as much studying as I can done while
riding, because I also started working part-time. Maybe it's
because I feel guilty about using money for school. Now I
work as a checker in a supermart ten hours a week. When
it is slow, the manager doesn't care if I take my books out.
Even though the girls aren't babies anymore, there is a lot
of work when I get home: cleaning, cooking, washing. But
the hardest part is keeping Al from feeling like less of a
man than he is. He has so many natural smarts."

Joanne's triple role as a mother/wife, student, and bread-
winner is overwhelming as she tries to perform each job
well. Our society pushes productivity. Women such as
Joanne often drive themselves unmercifully to prove their
worth. At the same time, they feel they must work hard to
preserve their husband's own sense of worth.

"The major hitch is that society and institutions are
doing little to help women chart new territory," says the
director of a women's studies program at one university.
"When a woman arrives for an eight o'clock class in the
morning, she has already taken someone to the train sta-

tion, done a load of laundry, taken out tonight's dinner from the freezer, and done myriad other activities.

"When a woman comes to me and tells me she is carrying fifteen hours, is a full-time housewife and mother, and has a part-time job, and is exhausted, but she can't give anything up because she has made a commitment, I say, 'Who said you can't back out now? You can.'"

The idea of being "superwoman" is a difficult one for many women to give up, and the problem of conflicting roles is not easily solved. Some of the following suggestions, however, may help you with this process:

1. Take stock of your priorities frequently. What you did six months ago may no longer be feasible. Learn to back away or drop an activity without guilt feelings. You are not a failure because you dropped a course to take a lighter load. Setting up a regular time for study doesn't mean you should *never* spend those important hours with a child or husband if you see they really need you. In other words, be flexible and learn to live with an unfinished task.

2. Continue to negotiate with your mate and children in the area of chores. Together, decide who is going to do what. "Where can I get the best food for the best price?" may be just the incentive to get your husband to do the shopping, and from that point, the cooking. Post all your schedules on a bulletin board. That way your family will know in advance when your exams are to take place, and you will know what important events of theirs you won't want to miss. Many role juggling problems are simply caused by faulty communication.

3. Support groups are one of the fine things to emerge from the women's movement. Thousands of them dot the nation, from chapters of the Center for Displaced Homemakers to Catalyst, a National Network of Local Resource Centers that lists more than 175 centers in the United States, many of them on college campuses. You will find that women returning to school face similar problems. Here you can find out how others have handled and perhaps solved your most pressing problem. One of us belonged to a

group that met in someone's home one evening every two weeks. It was a fluid group, and you could attend as you wished. One great lesson taught there was to learn to accept help from others; for example, pressing your mother or mother-in-law into service as the family cook when she comes to visit! Anytime you can motivate someone for unmet needs, you are exercising leadership.

4. *Flex-time* is a new concept in college and industry. Essentially, it means doing your job in the portion of the day/night/seven-day week that is reasonable for your life-style. In 1979, the state of New York became the first sizable public employer in the United States to offer alternative work schedules. A recent study found that it has resulted in increased productivity and opportunities for racial minorities, women, the handicapped, the elderly.

In some colleges, a full semester course is now offered for credit as a three-week mini-semester between regular semesters. In others, the identical course with the same instructor is offered in the daytime as well as in the evening session. Weekend college is a popular concept, too, with a spouse or family member filling in as sitter. You may want to press for more action in the area of flexible courses on your own campus.

Working toward a co-equal relationship with the other people in your life is a challenge but also a good feeling, as you grow closer through mutual respect and help. Although students and their families were always eager to discuss with us their problems as reentry students, they were overwhelmingly pleased with their decision to return to school. The pride in each other's accomplishments was expressed time and time again.

19

Facing Up to Problems in Personal Management

When we were returning students, fewer support services seemed to be available than there are today. We coped as best we could, made mistakes, and eventually solved some problems on our own. Today, colleges are more aware of the problems of returning students. Whether your problems are psychological, academic, personal, physical, or social, you can seek the assistance of trained members of the counseling and psychological centers on many campuses throughout the country. Even at Princeton University, where fewer than one hundred students are enrolled in the continuing education program, psychological services are available on the campus at the Health Center, and a brown bag lunch group allows students the opportunity to discuss transition problems.

We realize now that the most common kinds of problems we encountered were in personal management. In talking to other returning students, we learned about specific problems and weaknesses that seem to have some rather easy solutions.

OVEREXTENDING

We met Gary, an ex-Marine, in the cafeteria of a high-rise commuter college, where he was enrolled in a twelve-hour program.

"With my full-time job and full-time academic program, I just can't hack it," he said. "I'm failing my course in statistics." When we asked what he planned to do about it, he said he would just "brave it out."

Gary had alternatives. He could have dropped the hardest course without penalty or added another easier one to fill out the twelve-hour program. By making an early change to an easier course, Gary could have avoided endangering his GI benefits.

School counselors report that many students, especially returning veterans and scholarship recipients, frequently overextend themselves because they receive more pay for full-time attendance. When they do poorly, they become desperate and often plead with professors to change their grades. A few even offer bribes or try coercion to maintain the C average they are required to achieve.

Facing the problem of overextension often means merely making one change in your schedule.

FALLING BEHIND

Perhaps you have discovered that some of your courses are more demanding than you anticipated and you have fallen hopelessly behind.

Janet attended a college in the "frozen north," where the snow and sky seemed to meet in the winter. The field biology class she signed up for met at first in the warmth of the laboratory. Before the winter buds began to open, classes were moved outdoors in early March.

"Even though we were bundled up for the cold and snow, we shivered in below-freezing temperatures," she said. "The professor led us into a lonely woods or a bog where we could not retreat without fear of becoming lost. The three-hour classes would extend into overtime. When I spoke to the professor about my troubles, he suggested that I drop the course and try to complete, it in the summer months. It turned out to be an excellent suggestion. Exploring the summer countryside was an unforgettable experience."

You may have other reasons for failing to keep up with the class. Courses in math and science are building-block courses, and once you fall behind, you're lost. In other courses, reading requirements may be too difficult, the professor may be too demanding, or the lectures may be too abstract or misleading. Perhaps the fault is really yours.

What to do:

1. Make an appointment with the professor if you have been slipping academically in that course. Don't drop it until you have had a talk with the teacher, who may be able to give you some insights or explain some materials to you that will help you catch up.

2. Explain *why* you are falling behind; your professor may give you some special consideration. You can receive an incomplete grade for the course until you find the time to finish it.

3. Use a tutor. Services are free on some campuses, and on others a fee is charged by advanced students who offer tutoring services.

Face your problems while you still have alternatives available to you.

BAD DECISIONS

You could be well into a program before you discover you have made a bad decision in your career choice or course selection.

For example, Mary dreamed of being a pediatric nurse during the years she was raising her own small children. With two years of college to her credit, Mary enrolled in the nursing program at a local college. To her surprise, she discovered that some of the anatomy classes were upset-

ting. The math courses were also too difficult, and the idea
of becoming a nurse gradually seemed less attractive.

Seeking help from her counselor, Mary was advised to
change her major to special education. Now she is successfully pursuing her new career, which gives her more time
with her children and her husband. The new course of
study will give her the opportunity to express her love for
little children in a new way.

MIDLIFE TRANSITIONS

Harry worked for a steel company for thirty years. When
he retired in his early fifties, he decided to join the ministry
and entered a theology school in Delaware.

One of Harry's problems was adjusting from a logical
engineering approach in handling term papers to one of
open expression. He tended to look for specifics and iron-
clad reasons for expressing thoughts rather than an open,
free-minded style. Making the change from a career in
which he used pure logic and reason to the study of religion
and philosoply was indeed a giant step.

PHYSICAL AILMENTS

Dorothy was in her early sixties when she decided to get
her degree in fine arts.

"My problems were mostly physical ones," Dorothy said.
"My vision was poor, and while I was enrolled in a course
in humanities I had to have eye surgery. I reluctantly
realized that sometimes you are forced to come to a dead
stop and give yourself time to recuperate."

Dorothy showed the kind of perseverance needed to overcome obstacles. She was back in school after a few months
and was able to complete her work for a degree.

Events in your life may lay you low, but you have to be
ready to snap back with renewed spirit. Don't be discouraged by temporary setbacks. Professors generally cooper-
ate with you, often with great sympathy, when they know

about your physical problems. Be sure to call the professor's office in an emergency to keep your record straight. If your recuperation will be a long one, discuss your problems with your counselor, and ask her to tell your professors why you are not in class. You will certainly receive special consideration for work not completed and be given extra time when possible.

CULTURAL AND LANGUAGE PROBLEMS

Dionysia returned to school after more than forty years as a successful business woman. She had started work at fifteen, completing only one year of high school. "My greatest problem was English," she said. "How I prayed that I would do well writing papers. I don't know how I managed to receive Bs on most tests."

In the past few years, an increasing number of colleges have offered workshops in English for returning students like Dionysia. In addition, English as a second language has become a very popular course for students whose native or mother tongue is something other than standard American English. Both American and foreign students have taken advantage of these courses so they can learn or improve their English skills in reading, writing, and speaking.

INTERVIEW WITH SCHOOL PSYCHOLOGISTS

Dr. Gary Winderman is a psychologist at Bucks County Community College in Newtown, Pennsylvania. He notes several common problems of reentry students:

1. Anger: "Women returning students feel that they don't have the right to be angry in a relationship. They say, 'I should be the last person to be angry. Here I am, doing my own thing.' It's hard for them to feel deserving.

"The thing I stress all the time is that it is all right to feel anger. It is hard for people to understand the complexity of feelings that we are capable of at one time. They are immeasurable. I tell them to take the primary feeling and go with it. Say to yourself, 'I am feeling joy, anger, guilt, jealousy, but most of all, I guess I'm feeling angry, so I'll go with that."

2. Expectations: "What I often see in adult students is the feeling of anxiety about their performance. They have great expectations to do well. They will say, 'Now, don't expect me to do as well as some of the younger students. After all, I've been busy earning the bread or doing the bacon at home.' Yet they feel they *should* do better because they are older and more mature. There are great expectations on their parts. They are anxious about failure. Yet, in terms of basic skills, they are better at reading and writing and they think more clearly. They are typically bright or they wouldn't want to be in school."

3. Achievement: "Adult students seem to have high achievement needs or they wouldn't be here. Yet we have come to feel that achievement is a dirty word, that it isn't good to be achieving. I think we have to tell returning students that it is all right to want to achieve something, to be proud of it. It's all right to feel good about yourself."

SUMMARY

Inability to cope with problems can be regarded as *skills not yet learned*. If you can tackle your problems with the same kind of interest and desire for knowledge that inspired you to return to the academic world, you can overcome other problems, too. Norman Vincent Peale, in his book, *You Can If You Think You Can*, states that the only people without some kind of problems to solve are in the cemetery. Think of the challenge problem solving gives you, and the joy you feel when you conquer!

20

Other Help Groups

If your college has a "buddy system" for returning students, take advantage of the opportunity to have another adult student help you make the transition into college life. At some schools panels of peers have organized to meet and discuss transition problems with other returning students. Purdue has the Span-Plan Program; the University of Wisconsin has the Cracker Barrel group; and Bucks County Community College has the Stepping Stones organization, which provides a wide variety of services for returning students. These are just a few of the programs in effect now, but throughout the country, colleges are bending over backward to help returning students by developing peer counseling organizations.

HELP FOR SERIOUS PROBLEMS

Sherry was a returning student who enrolled in a three-hour course in history just to see if she could make it. "I have a lot of serious problems," she told us. "I hope going back to school will help me. I'm not sure I'm ready to take on more responsibility at this point."

Sherry indeed had problems. She felt she had failed at everything she had tried to do in life. In addition, her parents both died within a few months of each other; then she lost her job. Because Sherry was a student enrolled in a course at a college, she was able to receive excellent counseling from a psychologist on the school staff. In Sherry's case, the service was free.

If you feel that you can't cope with whatever problem is plaguing you, other services are available to you. Ask about the psychological service center or mental health facility on campus. In addition, many campuses have a crisis center or hot line. The latter operate on a twenty-four hour basis for students who have emergency situations they can't handle alone. Staffed by trained students and psychologists, they offer help with minor problems such as not being able to study, roommate strife, and lack of funds. Serious emergencies, such as rape, drug overdose, or emotional traumas, will receive prompt attention through the crisis center staff members. There is no way to trace your call; so if you simply need a listening ear, call and talk out your problems with a caring person.

ABUSED SUBSTANCES

You are trying to accomplish a lot as a returning student. If you are coping with added pressures with the aid of an addictive substance, you are in trouble. Although the term *abused substances* can apply to any drugs you use—aspirin, painkillers, uppers, downers, marijuana; also to food, alcohol, tobacco, sugar, or caffeine—it is your body and mind that are really being abused.

Have you lost control of your habit? Does it interfere with your normal functions on your job, at school, or in your social life? Are you emotionally dependent on that substance? If you can answer yes to any *one* of the three questions above, *you are addicted.*

At an eastern university workshop, Cathy spoke about her addictions. "My kids think I'm disgusting. They are teenagers, and they are in sports, run, eat health foods, and don't drink or smoke—*anything!* I'm not only addicted to cokes, cigarettes, alcohol, and coffee; I love gambling, too."

Although unaware of it, Cathy was taking the first step in overcoming her addictions: honesty about herself. She was admitting that she was not in control of her life or her habits. As Cathy reported, if she didn't have coffee, she got headaches; without alcohol, her hands trembled; and she had to have a cigarette on the way to the bathroom in the morning.

Psychologists call people like Cathy addictive personalities. She had cross-addictions that made her problems increasingly difficult. What she needed to find out about herself was why she needed all those anesthetics to make her life bearable.

Psychologists say that in chemical abuse—alcohol and drugs—something *is* to be gained from therapy. The first step is to be drug free, to be psychologically free from dependency. Alcoholism and drug addictions are diseases. A person with an alcohol addiction should improve in a stable supportive environment such as Alcoholics Anonymous. In some areas, people who are deeply involved in drug abuse are referred to other assistance groups, such as halfway houses like the "Today" program in Bucks County, Pennsylvania.

The National Institute on Alcohol Abuse and Alcoholism has published an excellent book about helping students with drinking problems. Write for *The Whole World Catalogue,* Care of the NIAAA at 5600 Fishers Lane, Rockville, MD 29852, and enclose $2.15.

Here are some of the rewards of overcoming addictions as promised by Alcoholics Anonymous:

- Hope instead of desperation
- Faith instead of despair
- Courage instead of fear
- Peace of mind instead of confusion
- Self-respect instead of helplessness
- Respect instead of pity and contempt
- A clean conscience instead of a sense of guilt
- Real friendships instead of loneliness
- A clean pattern of life instead of purposelessness
- Love and understanding of our families instead of doubts and fears
- Freedom of a happy life instead of bondage and obsession

21

Effective Complaining

We hope you never have occasion to complain during your return to school. However, if you do find a problem of real concern, consider its correction not only a personal obligation, but an obligation to the system to make it work well. Unsafe building conditions, harassment of any sort, inept teachers, and bad courses are more easily handled by mature, experienced students. No one is going to "get you" if you effectively communicate your concerns.

One timid returning student notes, "I would have to get at least two more degrees before I developed the confidence to complain." A professor in a prestigious university responds, "I've had two women reentry students. They were distinctive in that they refused to put up with garbage. They would try to circumvent any university rule that didn't make sense to them. The bad side is that their self-assurance includes the way they see the world. It is hard to convince them that there may be other ways of viewing the world."

Somewhere between these two types of students are the ideal college consumers, those who will stand up for what they believe is right, but who are also willing to see the other side.

Complaining is troublesome. It takes time, energy, and know-how, plus emotional commitment. There is always an additional consideration: Is it worth the social repercussions in terms of possible ill will and reputation?

"In the last few years students have a tendency to file grievances about everything," complains one faculty member who feels her colleagues are unduly attacked. Professors also charge that students with academic problems, resulting in confrontations, are not willing to face their *own* weaknesses.

Nevertheless, learning to confront the negative situation in your college career is one way that you learn who you are and one way to learn about the people and institution around you. The hurt you might encounter is that you won't get your way. Most of the time students think some terrible catastrophe is going to strike. You can express yourself even in sensitive areas without the roof falling in.

Paul W. discovered this when he found himself in a class of eight students, four of whom he thought were very poor students. "One seemed to copy everything out of a book for his daily presentation," he said. "I told the instructor I wasn't interested in having the book read back to me when I had just read it the night before. 'I'm wasting my time,' I told her. The result was she let me do my work outside of class because she felt obligated to help the others."

From our experience and investigation, we found that teachers are generally grateful, especially early in the course, if you tell them in a pleasant way how you feel about its shortcomings. If you tell them at the end of the course, it is too late to correct the problem.

Sometimes you may not be certain that your problem justifies a confrontation. A counselor in a graduate program at the University of Wisconsin says both male and female students talk to her—sometimes for several hours—to determine whether their problems should be aired beyond her office. "Just getting it off their chests may solve the problem," she explains.

Counselors can act as mediators, too. A student in a

community college accused an instructor of treating returning students in a "demeaning way, not treating them as
adults." The director of counseling talked with the instructor, chairperson, and divisional director, which resulted in
an attitude change. Here are some other examples:

- An instructor did not bring a sufficient number of
  copies for a final exam. Certain students were required to wait. They complained. Result: grades
  were revised upward.
- A teacher had not provided proper safety measures
  in a chemistry laboratory. An older student complained and the defects were immediately corrected.
- A professor who considered himself an amusing
  fellow posed people in the class according to whim,
  so that the sun might shine on someone's hair and so
  forth, to complete his tableau. An informal complaint
  was lodged through a dean, and he no longer does it.

FEARFUL STUDENTS

Every school has a prescribed set of rules to initiate
grievances. In most instances, they request that the student
confront the offending party or agent first. Some students
are afraid of retaliation. Others are just plain scared. They
are frankly intimidated by professors and titles. Psychologist Robert Alberti speaks about the strong tendency in our
society to classify people on a scale that makes some
"better" than others, using the following assumptions:

- Bosses are better than employees
- Men are better than women
- Adults are better than children
- Physicians are better than plumbers
- Teachers are better than students

We wonder why we should get special treatment when

we are not as smart or educated as the other fellow! The *Chicago Tribune* reports in a recent survey of 348 Chicago adults receiving help from others in the last four years that only half felt they had a "right" to help from co-workers, family, and friends when needed. One in four didn't even feel the right to ask for help from a professional person who would be paid for the service. Though many hoped for personal, warm relationships with professionals, few really expected this kind of emotional support.

Universities today, pressured by the human potential movement, human rights movement, women's liberation movement, and civil rights movement, have never been more amenable to addressing themselves to student grievances. Everything is in your favor.

If you still feel uncomfortable about speaking up, get help from the counseling office. They might even engage in role playing with you. For example, if you are not satisfied with the quality of your class, a role-playing session might begin with something like this: You say, in a firm but nonhostile voice, "When I entered this course I had the following expectations: . . . To date they haven't been met satisfactorily. I wonder if I am missing something. I really expected a tremendous challenge."

If the direct approach does not work, explain the situation to the personnel department, the dean, or the affirmative action administrator. Perhaps one of these parties can handle it without creating the disturbance you fear.

Although we suggest a ladder approach to voicing complaints, it is not unusual for students to go right to the top—the president, provost, or governing board. Those complaints always go back to the original source for clarification. One provost said he shoots complaints right back to the dean if they have not been aired there first. It is interesting to note, however, that he writes them down in his little black book and personally follows them up within a week.

We believe in complaining. How you present your complaints is crucial to getting good results. Here is how you can make them count:

1. Have your facts straight. If your complaint deals with grades, review the criteria utilized by the professor in grading students.
2. Allow for computer error and human error. Grades *can* be recorded incorrectly. The computer is a dummy. You are not.
3. Gather information or evidence and be knowledgeable. When the issue is grades, bring in all of your graded papers and note any other accomplishments.
4. Be timely with your complaints. Memory dims and distorts.
5. Find the correct-level person. Never deal with anyone who doesn't have the authority to give what you want.
6. Make photocopies of evidence and keep a careful record of pertinent telephone conversations.
7. Be explicit about what you want done.
8. If you are still not satisfied with the outcome, take your complaint to a government agency, a help or action center sponsored by a newspaper, or a lawyer.
9. Finally, be assertive—not aggressive. Assertion relies on the fact that most people react sensibly when a problem is pointed out to them. We found that true in academia.

22

The Law and You

An assistant professor of philosophy at a California university was dismissed after five female students accused him of fondling them, embracing them, and making sexual propositions to them.

A federal judge ordered a university in Tennessee to grant recognition to a student homosexual rights group under First Amendment rights. The university had refused to recognize The Student Coalition for Gay Rights.

In the not-so-distant past, colleges and universities were always "right." At the same time, women were often afraid to report incidences of sexual harassment. Now all that has changed. School administrators must think carefully about issues that infringe on student and faculty rights before they take a position. As a returning student you will find information in college handbooks spelling out your rights and procedures for grievances. You may never have a serious problem that cannot be solved inside the door of your counselor's or professor's office. Nevertheless, as a good educational consumer, it is important to know your rights under the rules of the university and the law.

Universities, by their nature, have always harbored non-conformists in the ranks of students and faculty. Thomas Jefferson, a founder of the University of Virginia, wrote in 1825:

> Our University goes on well. We have passed the limit of 100 students some time since. As yet it has been a model of order and good behavior, having never yet had occasion for the exercise of a single act of authority. We studiously avoid too much government. We treat them as men and gentlemen under the guidance mainly of their own discretion. They so consider themselves and make it their pride to acquire that character for their institution.

A few months later Jefferson wrote that the selfsame gentlemen, "animated with wine," masked themselves and ended their frolicking by throwing stones at some of the faculty. Jefferson records the outcome as follows:

> They were desired to appear before the Faculty, which they did. On the evidence resulting from this inquiry three, the most culpable, were expelled; one of them, moreover, presented by the grand jury for criminal punishment (for it happened that the district court was then about to meet). The eleven other maskers were sentenced to suspensions or reprimands, and the fifty who had so gratuitously obtruded their names into the offensive paper retracted them, and so the matter ended.

In Jefferson's time and for more than a century afterward, the concept of *in loco parentis* (the school is a substitute for the parent) persisted. Starting in the '60s, primarily due to the protest of students on the campus, institutions began to change.

This movement began in earnest in the year 1965, when John and Mary Beth Tinker were suspended from school by their Des Moines, Iowa, principal for wearing black armbands to protest the Vietnam War. Students and their parents sued to have the rule declared unconstitutional in the case of Tinker v. Des Moines Independent School District. Several years later the majority of the U.S. Supreme Court justices ruled in their favor.

The Tinker decision has had a monumental effect on students' rights cases. It has been the controlling precedent in almost every major state and federal case concerning the rights of students or teachers to freedom of speech and association.

Even before its resolution, a joint committee comprised of representatives from the Association of American Colleges met to formulate new principles of standards on the rights and freedom of students in higher education. Known as the *Joint Statement on Rights and Freedoms of Students,* its tenets are subscribed to by most of the academic institutions in the country, both private and public.

Since that time new legislation has evolved, giving students even greater protection under the law. In 1974, the Family Educational Right and Privacy Act (FERP) was signed into law by the President of the United States. FERP, which assures confidentiality of student records, forced every institution to develop a written policy of procedures covering the privacy rights of currently enrolled students. Here are the major provisions of the law that you, as a returning student, should be aware of:

1. *No one outside the university may have access to your records without your written consent.* If a prospective employer inquired about your class rank or grades, nondisclosure would be honored by the university until otherwise notified by you in writing.

2. *Inside the university only those persons or departments acting in your educational interest are allowed access to your records.* These might include offices of admissions, the registrar, and the vice-president of academic affairs.

3. *You may physically inspect and review information contained in your records and under most circumstances*

have copies made of them. This does not apply to confidential letters and recommendations associated with admission, employment, or job placement.

4. *You have the right to challenge the record on the grounds that its content is misleading, inaccurate, or otherwise in violation of your privacy or other rights.* You must be notified of the hearing within an appropriate time. You have the right to attend the hearing and to be represented by another person. You may choose a lawyer at your own expense and witnesses in your behalf.

If the notifications of the decision is unsatisfactory to you, you can place your own comments and reasons for disagreeing and this becomes a part of the permanent records. Furthermore, if you believe your rights have been abridged under the protection of FERP, you may file a complaint against the offending school with the Department of Education, 400 Maryland Ave. S.W., Washington, DC 20202; phone, 202-426-6573.

Although confidentiality in student records, the right of students to be free of arbitrary judgments, and the right of due process in disciplinary cases are covered by constitutional law, new issues have arisen in the '80s that continue to test students' rights. "The Constitution comes to the campus" has definitely created an atmosphere of "university beware."

PART V:
STUDY SKILLS

Introduction

When I speak of knowledge,
I mean something intellectual,
Something which grasps what it perceives
Through the senses;
Something which takes a view of things;
Which reasons upon what it sees
And while it sees;
Which invests it with an idea.
                              John Henry Cardinal Newman

One of the greatest fears of returning students is the inability to study effectively. Because of the gap of years since their last school days, they have forgotten the study skills.

"All I have had to remember are shopping lists and doctor's appointments," one returning housewife lamented. "I'll have to learn to use my brain all over again."

A business manager who had been in the business world for more than ten years said, "I've had a lot of experience in problem solving, but now that I'm enrolled in the M.B.A. program, I will have to study hard to bring home some good grades. Aside from my own expectations, my wife and kids will be expecting me to excel."

Yet older students need not be so apprehensive. Working

150

and accepting responsibilities, involvement in organizations, and the demands of everyday living have not only
provided the older student with maturity, they have also
encouraged greater determination and more intense moti-
vation. Learning to study again should be an easy task.

If your interest in a subject is not great in the beginning,
give yourself time. Think of the purpose of a course in the
field of study you have chosen and how you will apply the
course materials in a professional way in the future. If you
are still baffled by the purpose of the course, try to realize
that a good education will lead you into areas in which
your interest is limited.

Use all your senses when trying to grasp difficult studies.
In this case reading out loud and taking notes will put your
brain to work more completely. Underline main ideas,
concepts, supporting ideas, and unfamiliar words to help
you impress them on your memory and convince you of
their importance.

YOUR BODY AND YOUR STUDY HABITS

Increase the blood flow to your brain by exercising.
Stand on your head or put your feet up on a chair and let
the rest of your body rest on the floor.

Stay in good health. Poor health prevents you from
achieving your goals. Get a lot of rest, eat properly, and
exercise each day. Your harmful addictions will be replaced
by healthful habits if you take care of your body. Try
meditation, yoga, or running to improve your powers of
thinking.

Throw away the addictive substances that prevent you
from using your brain's fullest capacity. Nothing can slow
you down like poor eating habits, improper nourishment,
addictions to alcohol and harmful substances. Take care of
your internal ecology. Your brain will respond favorably.

If you do become blocked and overloaded with information, don't panic. This is the time to put your material on

the back burner of the mind where the unconscious, like a friendly collaborator, shifts and repositions data. Writer Conan Doyle knew how the process worked. In the middle of a case Sherlock dragged Watson off to a concert. Take a walk, relax with a nap, or play some tennis. Deliberately turn your attention elsewhere.

We have included study methods in greater detail to give you ideas on how to be a more successful student. You will find information devoted to improving your listening, reading, writing, research, critical thinking, memory, and other skills.

23

Memory and Imaging

Memory is the companion, the tutor, the poet, the library with which you travel.

Mark Van Doren

One fear often expressed by returning students concerns their lack of memory. "On the first day of my return to college," recalls Harry Morgan, a business student, "I forgot my house keys and thought, if I can't remember simple things, how am I going to remember accounting?"

Returning students admit to nervousness and fear of failing their first exams. They not only worry about what questions will be asked; they also wonder whether they can remember the facts they learned, and rightly so. Forgetfulness produces stress and is a costly problem in terms of time and performance. It also affects class discussion since you are less likely to speak up if you are afraid you may forget important points.

Inability to remember names can also hinder friendships, leaving your classmates coded as "the woman with the big glasses" or "the man with the red beard."

Although memory has been the subject of intense research for years, comparatively little is known about how

153

the mind remembers. What is known, however, is that memory does not deteriorate with age. Like the muscles of the body, memory only grows flabby with disuse. With practice, any healthy individual using simple memory techniques can increase the ability to retrieve information.

As a student you will find it desirable to forget a variety of things that do not fit your agenda. Doctor Hans Selye, one of the great pioneers in the field of stress, says:

> There is a limit to how much you can burden your memory; and trying to remember too many things is certainly one of the major sources of psychological stress. I make a conscious effort to forget immediately all that is unimportant and to jot down data of possible value (even at the price of having to prepare complex files). Thus I manage to keep my memory free for facts which are truly essential for me.

Mainly, you will want to improve your recall of general knowledge—a foreign language, accounting principles, a chemical formula, or whatever your course work offers.

One current and popular theory of memory states that there are certain "levels of processing," which means that your memory of a particular thing depends on how well the information was learned and organized to begin with. Items that are processed superficially won't be remembered as well as items that are processed when you are totally involved. Interest, enthusiasm, even fear can intensify the memory process. In this chapter we will look at personal attitudes, mnemonics (memory systems), and imaging as strategies to aid that involvement.

ATTITUDES

Probably the most overlooked and simplest means of enhancing your memory is to preface the information with the words *remember this.* You can consciously will memory.

In an experiment, students who were given a list of numbers without comment remembered far fewer than those who were given a similar list with instruction to remember them. Similarly, when a professor prefaces a statement in class by saying, "Make a note of this," or goes to the board to jot down a special word or formula, his inference is that an important fact is coming up and you better remember it. Prudent students stop daydreaming and focus their attention.

Because so much of our daily living is very automatic—driving a car, preparing dinner, catching the 8:05 train, buying a newspaper at the same newsstand—we tend to take attention for granted. Awareness of conscious attention to information is a critically important part of human memory. You can improve your memory simply by saying, *"This is important; I must remember this."*

You can also encourage a state of mind that will be conducive to remembering. It is generally believed that *mild* stress will improve the learning or encoding phase of memory. Is there anyone living at the time who does not remember exactly what he or she was doing upon hearing the news of Pearl Harbor or of President Kennedy's assassination?

According to Dr. James McGaugh, a psychobiologist at the University of California at Irvine, an increased emotional level triggers the release of chemicals in the brain that strengthens the synaptic connections that etch memory deeply. One of the reasons young people seem to have better memories is that they are excited and stimulated about the world around them. This heightened sense of excitement certainly applies to the returning student as well. Make it work for you in learning new material.

Conversely, a relaxed state of mind and body can aid in the recall of information. How many times have you totally blanked out on someone's name, growing more anxious as the person approached you with outstretched hand, only to remember it later while raking leaves or drinking a cup of coffee? Stress makes actors forget lines and dazes students during examinations. Whatever can be done to eliminate that stress—better preparation, experience, a time lag between learning and testing—will help you with recall. If you are tense, tired, or emotionally upset, forget it!

So, the first principle of memory is: heightened perception or slight stress helps you *learn*; relaxation helps you to *recall*.

Another strategy involves using your senses—all five of them, if you can. People tend to use one sense that predominates in their approach to remembering. Early exposure to problem solving probably determines your bias toward sense modality, but that can be changed, as we shall see later when we discuss visual image training.

Psychologists have shown that recall for writing is best achieved by ear-coded information, and recall for speaking is superior if coded by the eye. Keep this in mind when studying for exams or preparing for a talk. A group discussion would be helpful before a written examination, or even talking to yourself out loud; writing out what you want to say or running it through a typewriter would be helpful for your talk.

A theater director we know says you can tell what sense actors rely on when they study their lines. The *visiles* write down their lines; the *audiles* listen to their lines on a tape recorder; and the *tactiles* move around the room, waving hands for emphasis, touching objects, and so on, as a prompter feeds them lines they commit to memory.

Decide which sense you rely on most heavily while learning. If it doesn't seem to be working for you, resolve to try others.

Speaking of the theater, you can improve your memory by becoming a secret actor or actress. Memory expert Jay Walman of New York, a teacher of memory improvement for fifteen years, suggests using *emotions* to aid recall. Find an emotion—anger, happiness, joy, sadness—that fits the material and memorize it with that emotion. A talk to persuade your classmates would be practiced in a persuasive mood, as opposed to a clergyman's eulogy produced in a reflective tone.

He also suggests re-creating the setting as faithfully as possible while you are learning. Will your exam be written at a desk or at a long conference table, or will it be given orally while standing? Practice in the appropriate setting at home.

Robert Sommer, psychologist and author of *The Mind's Eye,* allows students to bring textbooks into class during examinations. Though they may not open them, students report that the presence of the material nearby allows them to re-create the image of the answer more readily.

Plan also to organize any material before you begin to memorize. Learning or encoding is just another name for the organizational process. By dividing information into chunks of facts, we tend to remember them. Imagine, for example, how difficult it would be to remember phone numbers or social security numbers if they were not separated with dashes into chunks of numbers.

Students have their own way of learning new information. One woman reports keeping cards with French vocabulary words in her car. Each time she comes to a stop, she repeats them out loud. In effect, as repetition and rereading occur at intervals, greater pattern recognition and extraction of meaning develop. Another student says, "I try to remember middle items. So often we remember the first or last."

MNEMONIC TECHNIQUES

Mnemonics, taken from the Greek word *mneme,* to remember, originated with Roman orators as a technique that enabled people to recite long speeches from memory with perfect accuracy. One powerful method they employed was the method of *loci.* Recall was accomplished by placing information in rooms of a mental memory house and then visualizing each location to retrieve it.

During the Renaissance, the eminent scientist and philosopher, Sir Francis Bacon, constructed a "memory theater" in his 17th-century house. Its window panes were painted with animals and birds in correct zoological order.

With proliferation of books, however, memory training fell into disfavor and became associated with the alchemist and his bag of tricks.

Today, mnemonics are being studied seriously by many psychologists. Donald A. Norman, psychologist and author of *Memory and Attention,* says, "Mnemonic systems provide us with the rules and techniques for shortening the sequence to be learned and finding meaning, even when there appears to be none."

One professor at a midwestern university gives students credit toward a course in memory and learning if they can demonstrate the use of a memory system. They are required to remember twenty-five words with 95 percent accuracy or better. "Not everyone is going to be excited about a memory system, but everyone is capable of using one," he says.

Most memory systems depend on making connections and associations in a purposeful way. The more ridiculous and outlandish, the better. One student recalls meeting the Newberry Award–winning children's author, Maia Wojcie-chowska, at a lecture. The author immediately informed the audience that her name was pronounced, "watch-your-house-key." The name, needless to say, is still remembered.

Verbal and Visual Systems

Acronyms such as NAACP, TWA, HOMES (the Great Lakes), IBM, and countless others are embedded in our language so deeply that we have almost forgotten what they stand for!

Favorite Sayings

"Every good boy does fine" (EGBDF) helps people remember the musical scale. A time-honored way of remembering the wrist bones has medical students memorizing this ditty: "Never lower Tilly's pants; grandmother may come home" (navicular, lunate, triquitrum, pisiform, greater multangular, lesser multangular, capitate, and hamate bones).

Peg Words

These have proved to be a useful memory system and are probably superior for remembering correct serial order. A *verbal rhyme* is made by pairing a number and an object: "One is a bun, two is a shoe, three is a flea, four is a door, . . ." By associating the visual image for each peg word with the item to be learned, you can remember a quantity of material. For example, if you were to remember each state in the United States, you might begin by visualizing the state of Washington sitting on a bun, Idaho sitting in a shoe, Montana swallowed by a flea. All very preposterous, of course, but consistent with the theory that learning or encoding is aided by a vivid encounter.

Our space is too limited here to recount all the possible or popular memory systems. For further information you may wish to read a best-selling book by Harry Lorayne and Jerry Lucas, *The Memory Book*. Meanwhile, try your own coding system that ties items together and integrates them into phrases, sentences, stories, or images.

Visual Imagery Training

To boost your memory power, you must learn to make your own strong images. Since studies show that visual memory provides a powerful alternative to memory associated with verbal associations, learning to use your mind's eye can be of tremendous help in your college work.

Novelists and magazine writers must have excellent powers of observation so that they may see things clearly enough to conjure up strong images for the reader. They write about the *majestic spires* of the old church and the *sandpaper surface* of the country road—words that have a high sensory content.

For our purpose, we are interested in reproducing images

and structural visualization. In the first we bring back images of the immediate past or the far past—rules for conjugating verbs on yesterday's blackboard or a remembered house or face from the distant past, much like watching a movie we have seen before. In structural visualization we construct things in our minds—the four sides of a cube or a house from a blueprint—a skill used by scientists and engineers. These two forms of imaging are controllable and learnable.

Consider for a moment your own experiences with actually seeing what is around you. After driving through your neighborhood or to your place of work hundreds of times, are you still unable to remember the names of the surrounding streets or stores? Could you describe the face of the last person who rang your doorbell? There are many distractions in our modern society. Yet to develop images to improve memory it is essential to see with purpose. This can be achieved with practice.

Aldous Huxley, author of *Art of Seeing,* coined the word *flashing,* a practice for short memory recall that illustrates how seeing can be improved through this simple exercise.

An Exercise

Before you begin, put yourself in a relaxed mood. Stretch out comfortably or sit comfortably at a desk or table.

1. Look at a scene in your school or home environment— a blackboard, for example. Analyze individual components—color, ledge, eraser, smudges or words on its surface. Also see it as a single entity.

2. Close your eyes. Photograph with your mind's eye the clearest image possible of what you have just seen as you would on a blank TV screen.

3. Open your eyes and compare your image with the model.

4. Close your eyes once more and conjure up the image. Reopen your eyes and compare images a second time.

Repeat this a few more times and you will be surprised

at the improved clarity of your model. The principle here is: practice followed by prompt feedback will enhance seeing.

Visual thinking is not in the exclusive domain of the artist. Surgeons as well as architects, football coaches and chess players must think visually. Jack Nicklaus has said that before hitting a golf ball he always visualizes where he wants it to land.

You may want to try this exercise to improve structural visualization. Choose an imaginary fruit or vegetable with an interesting inside. Put it up on the screen in your mind. Make an imaginary slice through its center. Now actually sketch each of the sides on paper. Repeat the process by bisecting the remaining halves and once again draw views of each quarter. Your drawing skill is not important.

Don't be disappointed if your initial attempt at conscious visualization is poor. With practice, you will improve and thereby improve recall and your ability to literally see a problem from all sides.

24

The Art of Critical Thinking

> You will find that truth is often unpopular and the
> contest between agreeable fancy and disagreeable fact
> is unequal. For, in the vernacular, we Americans are
> suckers for good news.
>
> Adlai E. Stevenson

As children, we learn to think through our senses and
through observation. When we grow older, our thinking
becomes more complicated, more symbolic, and we are able
to understand concepts.

A concept can be as simple as a thought or an opinion. It
is a mental image, a generalized idea formed by combining
the elements of a class into the notion of an object. Concepts are the basis of all human thinking, and they are used
at all levels of abstraction.

Harry Maddox, author of *How to Study,* describes the
child who, upon reaching out his hand to touch a lighted
candle and being burned, retracts his hand when shown a
lighted electric bulb. The child has conceptualized the idea
of luminosity and has generalized the idea that luminous
objects will burn him. The simple abstractions you make as
a child become more developed as you grow older.

Understanding basic concepts and theories makes it possible to adjust to changed conditions. In civil engineering and science, it is impossible to memorize every situation. It is necessary to understand the principles of their application.

For example, in a class in mathematics, while studying the principles of stress analysis, many students attempted to memorize the complex mathematical exercises required to analyze the stresses developed in a railroad bridge as an engine crosses from left to right. In an examination covering this subject, the professor brought the engine in from right to left and some students could not adjust to the changed condition.

You must understand certain fundamental cornerstones or building blocks in order to succeed particularly in engineering sciences and mathematics. And it is important to understand rather than memorize. One way to better understanding is to ask yourself questions.

Without being aware of it, you have used the basic approach to critical thinking in your daily life—asking questions. For example, when you purchased your last car, you asked the salesman, among other things, about gas and mileage performance, the size of the motor, the price. From the data received you then made your choice according to your own needs. The same format applies to hiring a babysitter or an assistant in your office.

Of course, you could dispense with the questions in both cases and make your choice on the basis of gut feeling. Intuition plays a definite role in problem solving, which we will discuss later, but now we are dealing with critical thought, which begins with a problem and a set of questions to provide information. In this case, which is the *best* car for the money? Who is the *best* applicant for the job?

Now that you are returning to school, most of your critical thinking will involve asking yourself the questions. What you have been doing routinely can become a powerful tool when applied to your college studies.

When we returned to school, we progressed from a weak

grasp of some subjects to a stage in which we had a more refined and powerful grasp of our materials. Initially we suffered anxiety and embarrassment from our state of ignorance. We were self-conscious about problem solving. Only as time passed did we realize problem making and problem solving were important processes of the learning experience, the area in which critical thinking is honed. One common piece of advice we learned to use with top efficiency was the basic "who, what, where, when, why, and how" method of inquiry for problem solving.

WHO, WHAT, WHERE, WHEN, WHY, HOW?

Research shows that our capacity for processing information is limited to six or seven unrelated ideas simultaneously. An excellent device for processing information is to file it according to the answers to "who, what, where, when, why, and how?"

This method if inquiry is so obvious that it seems it need not be explained, yet students compare it favorably with the invention of the wheel. We did. For one thing, it is a mode of inquiry that protects our thinking apparatus from overload. It is exquisite in its simplicity. Furthermore, it sets down fact and allows us to explore connections that before were unsuspected. For example:

> Several hundred persons were evacuated from the Tribune Tower Tuesday night when a fire started in the basement and spread through the ventilating system.

Glance at the first few paragraphs of any newspaper story. *Who, what, when,* and *where* are invariably at the beginning. Even if the editor should cut the story, the reader still has the basic facts.

Where do we get the facts? In books and other reference material, from people and organizations who can answer our questions, and from our own experience.

The *why* and *how* are more intricate questions. They

often refer to hidden, sometimes subtle, implications as distinguished from openly expressed facts. Gathering the facts relating to *who, what, when,* and *where* requires patience and acceptance. The *why* and the *how* require diagnosis and criticism; they are the toughest parts of the thinking process, the points at which we make connections about the facts and form a tentative argument or hypothesis suitable for testing against reality. To get the right answers, you must ask the right questions.

Question: What was the main reason the South lost the Civil War? After examining facts about each side's political, social, and economic condition and the conduct of its armed forces, your argument might be that the South lost because slavery was inherently evil and God was on the other side, or that Jefferson Davis was not as capable a leader as Abraham Lincoln, or perhaps that England and France would not recognize and aid the South. (All of these answers are true to some degree, though you would have a difficult time persuading an atheist of the first one.)

In making your analysis and drawing conclusions about the material you gather, you must be sure of the following:

1. Your judgments about the material are reasonable.
2. You have sampled enough facts to make a generalization.
3. The effects are indeed due to their causes.
4. Your conclusions are logical and realistic.

(Most authorities agree that the South lost because it lacked the manpower and the productive capacity for munitions and arms, while the North successfully mobilized and maintained a loyal citizen army.)

The biggest stumbling block to discovering good *hows* and *whys* is difficulty in isolating problems—separating the real basic problems from the merely apparent or distantly related ones. You must decide which relevant points are missing and which irrelevant points should be tossed out. As new information is gathered, you must also be willing to change your mind.

Critical thinking is difficult for many returning students, but it is the most important skill you can learn in college. You can retrieve facts from the computer, but the computer cannot tell you *why.*

So explore the facts, then find the answers whose truth suggests conformity to them. Here are five steps to follow in the problem-solving process, using your powers of observation and reason:

1. State the problem.
2. State the facts.
3. Explore the connections.
4. Generate solutions or theories to the problem.
5. Test for truth.

After all this, perhaps it seems like a paradox to say that truth is relative. The truth is that we can never hope to know all the truth; the closest we can come to it is probable truth, since our perception of a problem is determined by several factors outside our control.

FACTORS THAT INFLUENCE PERCEPTION

Personal History

We all experience things differently. We relate our sense data to our particular past experiences, knowledge, personality, and expectations. They filter information we receive. (We remember a student in a literature class responding to a poem by comparing its fiery images to the electric chair only to discover later her great uncle had died in one!)

Language

How we view a problem is further affected by our language and culture, which play strange tricks on us. How common is common sense? How united the United Nations? What does the word *freedom* mean to an Iranian, a

Russian, an American? The point is that we can never be totally objective because our language is not precise. Words mean different things to different people.

Imperfect Senses

We at least can trust to observation, verifying with our own eyes. Right? Not so, says researcher Robert Ornstein, author of *The Psychology of Consciousness.* He gives these examples of expectations of color and line experiences: "If we are 'ready' to see a black ace of spades or a red ace of hearts when a red ace of spades is shown, we will see one of the two choices we have set for ourselves. Or if we are in the same way 'ready' to make a straight eye movement in response to a curved line, we will see the curved line as straight."

Our memories are equally self-serving. We tend to remember the most vivid image—the blue jay, not the wren. Or we retain the pleasant memory that supports our own self-image—the winning tackle, not the bench.

Theories—Imperfect Laws

We tend to forget that a theory is only a formulation of general principles of observed phenomena that has been verified to some degree. Major opposing theories stand side by side, drawing their own cheering sections.

In educational psychology, Robert Gagne and Jean Piaget developed opposite theories about the way children learn. Gagne's research demonstrated that children, except for their very earliest years of life, can learn anything at any age, provided they have mastered the preceding step. Piaget, on the other hand, demonstrated that children learn specific skills at specific age intervals.

New evidence is always being discovered that causes major shifts in thinking. Darwin's theory of the evolution of man conflicted with the earlier biblical "truth" of man's beginnings.

Imperfect Authorities

Authorities are specialists in various fields of inquiry and often are the originators of what they profess. They, as well as lay persons, sometimes reason from unreliable premises. It is not unusual for them to disagree among themselves, as in the case of Gagne and Piaget. Neither is it unusual for them to fall from grace. The father of psychoanalysis, Sigmund Freud, suffered a diminished following when the humanistic school of psychology proliferated in the '60s and '70s. So beware of "dogmas" attributed to authorities unless they can stand on their own logic and evidence.

It is also important to remember that authorities are not limited to traditional academic scholarship areas—the university or laboratory. Ronald Gross, in his book, *The Life-long Learner,* offers repeated examples of "gifted amateurs" who found their own ways to important truths. They are the Thor Heyerdahls, Eric Hoffers, and Alex Haleys of the nonacademic world.

Whether you use the "who, what, when, where, why, and how" method or choose another model of inquiry that is appropriate to the material, you can become the thinking person you aspire to be. *Knowledge is an outcome of disciplined inquiry and can be pursued by anyone.*

25

Tips on Writing

Writing is an act of faith. Courage is the first essential.
Katherine Anne Porter

Writing favors the seasoned mind. Even if your current writing consists only of notes to the mailman, memos to an employee, or letters to a friend, you can become a competent writer. There are definite skills for writing research papers that are learnable, but first let's talk about writing in general.

People pick up a page of printed words with great expectations—even weary-eyed professors with piles of term papers on their desks. Since the advent of Gutenberg's press, millions of books have been published and have served as a source of pleasure and enlightenment. Readers want to come away from them enriched—armed with a new perspective, new information, and a feeling that the experience has been worthwhile.

How do you find interesting topics to write about for college essays when subjects are not assigned?

Contemporary social, political, and economic problems afford many lively issues for the writer. Which issues are the people *you* know talking about? What happened to you last week that keeps popping back into your mind? What will happen in the future—an election, a centennial celebration, a new development in the field of telecommunications?

Readers are intrigued by the largest, smallest, best, worst, highest, shortest of *anything*. They are also interested in themselves and in ways to improve their health, nutrition, sex lives, social lives, careers, and minds. They are fascinated by unique people and events.

Whether you are writing a business letter, a letter to the editor, an essay, or a term paper, choose a subject that interests you, but study your audience, whether it is an audience of one (your professor) or of one hundred.

MAKING IT LIVELY

Even the most technical and esoteric subjects can be enlivened with a sprinkling of examples, anecdotes, quotations, statistics, and comparisons. Dull writing is not necessarily the product of a dull mind, but rather a lazy mind. It takes a certain amount of thinking to gather the above evidence.

Uninformed writers will use elongated phrases like *at the present* instead of *now* and all kinds of windy jargon. ("I never write 'metropolis' for seven cents a word because I can get the same price for 'city,'" observed Mark Twain.) Although elegant words like *tome, volume,* and *publication* are sometimes appropriate, settle for *book* and see how well it works. If you think you are insulting your readers, remember that the prestigious *Wall Street Journal* and the *New Yorker* are written at an eleventh-grade reading level.

Speaking of words, be aware that words have a denoted meaning and a connoted meaning. The first is derived from the dictionary, the second from individual experience. Words like *snake, moonlight* and *gold* hold powerful images for the reader and speak of other things as well as their dictionary meanings. There are even funny words. Get ready to smile. *Prunes* is one of them.

For clarity's sake, stay with your topic. Your essay, report, letter, whatever, is like a train on a track headed for the home station. You can take small detours, but you must keep returning to the main track. Extraneous material—often padding or unrelated thoughts—will detract from the impact your main point should have, eliciting a loud yawn from your readers. Cut out unnecessary words or phrases at each step of writing.

New writers tend to pack too many thoughts into a single sentence for fear of appearing simpleminded. They also use too few sentences in a paragraph because they cannot think of enough to say. Sheridan Baker, in his book, *The Practical Stylist,* suggests planning for the big paragraph of four or five sentences by visualizing rectangular frames to be filled. With practice, you will soon be able to fill them with interesting details. Later, you can vary the size of your paragraphs.

Probably one of the best ways to know if you are writing clearly is to hear your work read aloud. We have participated in writers' workshops where this is done routinely. At these workshops we first encountered the responses "So what?" and "I don't get it" to prose that we had thought was effective and interesting. These are probably the most damning reactions an audience can have to a piece of writing, but they do point out to the author serious defects in the work.

WHAT ABOUT OUTLINES?

Using a formal outline is a systematic and workmanlike approach to the task of writing. The relationship between your ideas can be seen more easily in outline form. In the long run, writing an outline may save time and reduce the need to write multiple drafts.

One professor who teaches writing says, "I tell my students to write and write and never take their hands off the typewriter keys. Something will start to emerge. 'I never know what I know until I write it' is a fair statement to make. Students should not be afraid to engage themselves totally in the subject they are writing about. I couldn't care less about outlines and finding a theme. You find it when you write it!"

Our approach is somewhere in between. We find that a jot sheet is sufficient to help us organize our material. A jot sheet is exactly what the term implies. It is a loosely assembled group of words or phrases to note the important points of your material. It allows you the free, uninhibited thinking of a brainstorming session. Whatever method of organization you decide on to set your words in motion, make sure you are comfortable with it.

REVIEWING YOUR WORK

After composing the first draft of your writing, put it aside. The act of creating often causes a euphoria that conceals mistakes. Looking at it with a cold eye a few days later will show you where corrections are needed. This is also a good time to recheck for correct punctuation and spelling. When you are finished writing the first draft you might also reexamine your writing by asking yourself the following questions:

1. What am I trying to say?
2. Did I use the right words and examples to be effective?
3. Does the length suit the material?
4. Is it lively?
5. Did I allow for the thesis statement in the introduction, the main ideas and subordinate ideas in each paragraph of the body, and a summation or conclusion at the end?

Improve your writing skills, not only to present a better image of yourself in the classroom, but also to express your ideas in an orderly way. The act of writing is part of the learning process because it forces you to think things out, to synthesize, and to improve your reasoning powers.

THE RESEARCH PAPER

Researching for college papers is one of the most vital exercises in the college experience. It can be an adventure in which you are the detective looking for the clues and facts that will lead you to information.

Your work may begin when the professor reminds you that your research paper will be due in a few months. During the semester, you have been thinking about this assignment with a sense of dread or of pleasant anticipation. Perhaps a subject has been assigned to you, or several topics have been suggested. Your syllabus—usually issued at the first class meeting—should list these and other facts, such as the length of the paper, the number of resources, the requirements for the bibliography, suggested books and other source materials, and the exact date the paper is due, even the time limit in hours! (We remember one professor who had a time stamp, and his secretary timed the arrival of your paper in his office by the date, hour, and minute.)

Selecting a Subject

If you are given a list of subjects, select one in which you have some interest or special insights. Have you had some experiences that make you feel comfortable about one subject? Has another course given you some information or interest you would like to explore further? Be sure your chosen subject is narrow enough to give you a manageable concentration, yet broad enough to give you a good selection of resources.

Most professors expect you to write out a contract in which you state your research project or emphasis. For example: "For my research paper in genetics, I propose to write about the subject, 'Birth Defects in the Children of Racially Mixed Parents.'" "My research subject for English literature will be 'The Life and Work of Thomas Campion, Renaissance Poet.'"

Your subject may not be approved by the professor, in which case he will tell you why or even suggest a broader or narrower interest or focus. He may even suggest an entirely different subject and give you some leads on resources.

Most professors will expect you to present a typewritten, double-spaced paper, and in a style acceptable to their expectations. Be certain about what is expected of you before you begin your research.

Three important factors will concern you in a research paper:

1. Organization: gathering together all the information, then creating your own presentation in an organized way.

2. Documentation: noting all your resources according to book titles, authors, publishers, dates, sources on films, tapes, laboratory experiments, interviews, and other research methods. All your resources must be footnoted or end-noted on your paper. For information, consult Kate Turabian's books, *Students' Guide for Writing College Papers* and the more advanced *Manual for Writers of Term Papers, Theses, and Dissertations,* (both published by University of Chicago Press).

3. Presentation: Begin by making a thesis statement in the introduction. This will be the statement that indicates the purpose of your paper. In the body, present the facts you have gathered about the subject. Arguments for the acceptance of certain facts, as well as arguments against them, should be included. Add attitudes and personal insights about your subject that are well conceived and carefully thought out. Then end with a summary or conclusion that will include a closing statement to wrap it all up.

For highly technical or specialized subjects, the professor usually presents the student with a list of resources, such as books, tapes, periodicals, and films, that are often placed on reserve lists or shelves in the library. The librarian will set aside and maintain the list of these reserved books and materials at the request of the instructors. Usually, there is a strict time limit on taking out these sources because of the number of students who need the materials at the same time.

As an investigator, you have at your service some of the most resourceful, patient, intelligent helpers in the whole world: reference librarians. Just ask them a few questions and watch them beat the bushes for you.

If you feel overwhelmed by the writing process, consider taking a basic English composition course at your community college *before* you return to school. Another excellent course, whether you are headed for a business career or not, is a course in business communications that teaches report and letter writing.

Letter writing makes you analyze your reader and situation as they apply to the tools of business and psychology. A good letter can influence people by showing you at your best.

Report writing will teach you to do the research and documentation that are needed for general term papers. It can also be a great help if you decide to enter graduate school. If you have already learned how to collect, organize, and interpret data and to document your writing, your research papers and theses will be a lot easier to write.

26

How to Improve Your
Reading Skills

Read not to contradict and confute,
Nor yet believe and take for granted,
Nor to find talk and discourse, but
To weigh and consider.

Francis Bacon, from *Of Studies*

Many students do not read with the kind of speed and efficiency they could attain, and they fail to get full value out of their reading assignments. They stumble through the reams of reading materials, wishing they could concentrate, distracted by the pulse of life going on around them.

As a returning student, you may want to brush up on your reading technique. The ability to read rapidly and well, then to weigh and consider, is the secret of getting full value out of reading assignments, getting good grades, and ultimately enjoying your college years.

Your first consideration for improving reading skills should be to define your greatest problems. Only by becoming aware of what you are doing wrong can you start your self-improvement campaign. Do your eyes move back and forth along one line of print, trying to capture the meaning of the sentence? Does your mind wander while you are supposed to be concentrating? Do you voice the words or mumble under your breath? Do you read the words one by one? These are some of the negative habits students must overcome.

POINTERS FOR GOOD READING

1. Before you begin to read, think of the purpose you have in mind. Are you reading to form a critical opinion, to find facts, to search out new ideas or concepts? Or is your purpose merely to enjoy the craftsmanship of the writer?

2. Vary your reading speed with the kind of book you are reading. You will want to skim some assignments rapidly to cover a large amount of material in a short time. Other assignments will demand that you slow down to be deliberate and to observe more detail.

3. Learn to group words together:

Slow   readers   try   to   read   one   word   at   a   time.

To increase your speed,   read in groupings   or thought units   so you will be able   to read like this.

Gradually, the spaces between words   will become smaller until you are able   to have shorter spaces   between word groups or thought units.

As you become more proficient, your mind will be picking up thought units as your eyes move ahead.

4. Keep your eyes moving ahead. If you are distracted or inattentive, your eyes may keep moving back and forth on one line while you try to understand meanings. If you are thinking about some office intrigue, or trying to pay your bills, you will not really absorb what you are reading. Or, if you are a lazy reader, if your mind is not focused on the

print before you, your reading pace will be slower. In other words, *concentrate!*

5. Keep a dictionary at your side. Look up the definitions of words you don't know. While you are increasing your vocabulary, you are also increasing your speed. Your eyes will readily accept words whose meanings you have mastered. Like new friends, they add interest, subtlety, robustness, delicacy, and excitement to what could be rather dull prose.

6. Don't read aloud unless you are reading a special soliloquy in a play or serious poetry. If you verbalize, even subconsciously, it will slow you down and add hours to your reading time.

7. Learn to weigh and consider what you read. Let the meanings of the words sink into your consciousness. What are the facts? What are the main points and the supporting arguments and statements? Do you understand the message the author is trying to send? Do you agree with the author's statements? Make judgments. As you learn critical thinking and apply it to your reading, you are less likely to accept false ideas or concepts. You will learn to accept or reject the author's arguments.

8. Some words are like traffic signs because they create transitions. A few examples of the function of these transitional words follow:

- To add to, extend, or illustrate a point: *and, furthermore, also, or, nor, moreover, along with, similarly,* etc.
- To summarize: *consequently, therefore, finally, at least, afterward, until, no sooner, at once,* etc.
- To establish time: *now, then, usually, never, soon,* etc.
- To consider alternatives: *certainly, yet, however, but, still, notwithstanding, conversely,* etc.
- To link cause and effect: *as a result, because, inevitably,* etc.

- To refer back: *these, they, that, he, she, it, none,* etc.
- To restrict and qualify: *in the case of, provided that, only, if,* etc.

Immediate recognition and understanding of transitional words will increase your reading proficiency and be helpful when you write papers as well.

HOW TO READ A BOOK

Every book has a unique personality and point of view. In a way, it has the possibility of becoming an old friend. To start your relationship in a positive way, pick up the book and read its title page. There you will find the date it was published, the author's name and credentials. Scan the glossary of useful terms, the index, and the bibliography. Know what guides the author used that may also be of assistance to you.

Use the bibliography to investigate further your special interest in the book. These listed references may refer you to books, magazine articles, journal articles, diaries, and other writings the author has read to aid his own presentation. An appendix, though not always present in textbooks, contains material related to the work, but not necessarily suitable for inclusion in the main body. For example, explanations of methods, copies of documents, charts, and case studies may be found in the appendix.

HOW TO READ A CHAPTER

Sometimes you may find, for study or research purposes, that you are interested in only one or two chapters in a book. A good way to begin reading a chapter is to look at the table of contents to determine the relationship of the chapter to the outline of the complete book. Recognize the chapter as a unit of the book, a piece devoted to one topic. Now, turn to the chapter and study the title and subtitles and try to relate the divisions to the theme of the book. Read the introduction or first paragraph, the summary, and the conclusion. After making this quick appraisal, you are ready to begin at the introduction again; this time, however, you will read the entire chapter with greater speed and comprehension.

Most of your college reading will require close, analytical skills. Your speed will be regulated by the kind of materials you must comprehend. When reading an essay, you may be forced to read more slowly to understand the author's point of view and to consider his arguments and ideas. Factual materials cannot be read at a gallop, yet some readers prefer to read quickly through a chapter or section of a book to get the big picture, then reread it for details.

In a short time, your textbooks will become familiar objects to tuck under your arm with assurance. Reading with speed and skill is a gradual accomplishment, and the more you work at it, the faster you will learn.

27

Listening and Note Taking

He listens well who takes notes.

Dante

LEARNING TO LISTEN

Communication is a two-way process. It involves the *transmission* of information and the *reception* of information. Speaking and writing skills are thought of as the transmission of verbal communication, while visual and aural senses are involved in the reception of communication. *All* our senses are involved in the listening process.

LISTENING SKILLS

In order to listen well, you must be able to hear well. The art of listening also depends on intellectual and mental action. You must comprehend what you hear, then interpret and evaluate the message intellectually.

At one time, emphasis was placed on the area of attentive or concentrative listening. Now, however, the courteous, reactive, evaluative, and critical listening aspects are considered the most essential listening skills.

Concentration is necessary to listening effectively. The

most important aid to concentrating is the elimination of conscious or unconscious distractions or noise. What is heard must be perceived and given meaning, then it must be interpreted and evaluated.

Critical listening involves the ability to detect illogical thinking or inconsistencies and propaganda messages. Unless you have the advantage of recording on tape the lectures you attend, you must grasp the meaning immediately while listening to the speaker. Because our minds work faster than a speaker can speak, the difference in speed can be put to work in forming questions, taking notes, or adding your insights to the material.

College courses in the art of listening are being offered at the University of Minnesota, Western Michigan University, University of California at Santa Barbara, Bradley University, and many others. Listening skills are also being taught in conjunction with courses in speech.

NOTE-TAKING METHODS

We have been making notations all our lives, jotting down important facts—in essence separating the wheat from the chaff. Now that you are returning to school, learn some note-taking skills in advance. You will see that notes represent a major source of information to be reviewed before examinations as well as a separate learning experience.

It might be a good idea to sit down in front of your television set with pen and paper in hand. Tune in a station whose format approximates a lecture, perhaps a program on your educational channel or a news report. Now listen carefully and take notes. How did it go? Probably not too well, unless you have been away from school for only a short time or you are a professional secretary. Study the following suggestions for improving your note-taking skills:

1. Have a looseleaf notebook or a section of a notebook for each class.

2. Write down the date of the lecture on top of the page so that you can refer to it when conferring with others.
3. Allow wide margins on your pages for comments that you can fill in later after additional readings or lectures.
4. Copy important definitions, quotations, and formulas word for word, but state other information in your own key words. Try to digest what the lecturer says as he speaks.
5. Give visual emphasis to important ideas underlying key statements. Use asterisks, arrows, and different-colored inks.

FOR OPTIONAL LEARNING

Review your notes and rewrite them as soon as possible, probably within the next twenty-four hours. Studies show that students typically forget about 60 percent of new material within this time span. By rewriting notes you have an opportunity while they are still fresh in your mind to add examples and facts that you did not have time to write down during the lecture.

Not enough people make up a personal shorthand system that can be used for note-taking under pressure. Why write out *approximately* when you can use the abbreviation *approx.* and save time. By dropping some vowels or consonants, words can be shortened without confusion. Some examples are: *govt, democy, natl, biol,* etc. Do not overdo abbreviations. The letters *com* could be community, communism, committee, and a lot more. Standardize the ones you use often. Here are some standard symbols:

> more than	⌢ over
< less than	⌣ under
→ leads to, results in	∴ because
← comes from, cause	∴ therefore

For a very important lecture, which you know about in advance, you might want to bring a battery-powered tape recorder to class and sit as close to the lecturer as possible. Taping allows you to listen intently. Afterwards, take notes from the tape. Recording lectures from tape is a great study aid because you can repeat entire lectures or replay only the sections you wish.

Be a flexible note taker. That means exchanging your notes with others. Be careful about giving your *only* notes away. You and your fellow students may want to go to the copying machine together to make duplicates.

28

Tests, Techniques, and Skills

Technique is hardly worth talking about unless it's used
for something worth doing.

Pauline Kael

An important measurement of your success as a returning student is your ability to get good grades on your tests.
In addition to the personal esteem involved in maintaining
a good grade point average, educators and future employers will use your test scores to determine your fitness to
enter graduate school or to be accepted as an employee.

Yet, according to Bernard Feder (*The Complete Guide to
Taking Tests*) and other authorities, grades are not necessarily a true measure of your knowledge of a subject.
Rather, they prove your skill in test taking. Although a
great deal of controversy is raging at this time in the
American testing system, the fact is that knowing how to
prepare for and pass tests as they exist today is a major
academic skill.

PREPARING FOR A TEST

All semester long you have been studying, taking notes,
reviewing, attending lectures, organizing your material,

and concentrating on the content of the course of study. Whether the test you are taking is a final exam or a mid-term, you want to do your best. Since a large percentage of your grade for the course will be based on your test scores, you must give yourself every available advantage, not only in preparation, but in knowing what to expect in the testing procedures.

Make a special effort to attend your classes during the week before a major test, no matter what might stand in your way. Usually, professors will tell you the type of test they intend to give. They may review the test materials during class time or will tell you what areas the test will cover.

While preparing for an essay test, look for trends and themes as you study. Try to anticipate the kinds of questions the test will contain. Review the main ideas and supporting ideas of your subject, then restate them in your own words. Ask yourself about the important principles; questions that you think require statements; include other important information or details, using questions of varying degrees of difficulty. Be prepared to express your own opinions or positions and support them with evidence.

TAKING THE TEST

On the day of the test, you should allow extra time to get to class ahead of schedule. This will give you the advantage of being settled before you start the exam. In addition, the professor may have some information or instructions that will help make the test easier for you.

Before you start, survey the entire test and be sure you know exactly what is required. Follow the directions very carefully and budget your time according to the value of the questions. Answer the easiest questions first. If you have any options, choose the questions with which you feel most comfortable. Leave plenty of space for answers you have omitted and for additional thoughts you may want to include.

In essay tests, words of instruction may have totally different meanings. Be certain that you know exactly what is expected of you.

1. Describe or analyze: Other terms used are *define, review, enumerate, develop, trace, outline,* and *summarize,* all of which are other ways of describing and analyzing.
2. Explain or prove: Other terms used are *interpret, comment, state,* and *discuss,* all of which are ways of explaining or proving.
3. Make a personal judgment or evaluate: Other terms used are *criticize, interpret,* and *justify.*

You will note that some of the instructional words listed above are used in all essay questions. They are designed to describe and analyze, explain or prove, etc. If you are in doubt of the directions for an essay test, ask questions immediately. The professor or test official will be waiting to clarify the instructions.

If you get a mental block and freeze up, try to start writing thoughts that come into your mind about the subject. The very act of writing seems to increase your chances of remembering "lost" information. Know exactly what is expected of you before you begin to write. If you don't know the answer to a question, try to reason it out. You may receive partial credit for some answers, but be certain that wrong answers are not counted against you. If they are, answer only the questions of which you are reasonably sure. Try to keep your statements brief and concise.

Make a concerted effort to ignore your neighbor while you are taking tests. A casual question or a whispered remark, even if it's just about borrowing a pen, could leave you open to charges of cheating, penalties, or expulsion from the test. If you have problems, raise your hand and ask the professor for assistance. This also applies when a classmate is trying to ask you about something. Never take notes to class during a test, and don't cheat. A grade that is earned, good or bad, is a measurement of your progesss and understanding.

When you have finished the test, check your paper to determine if you have completed all the answers to your satisfaction. Are your statements clear and concise? Are all spelling and grammatical errors corrected?

TAKING OBJECTIVE TESTS

Objective tests are also known as short-answer tests. They are completion tests, true-false tests, matching question tests, multiple-choice exams, or a combination of several or all of these tests. The greatest difficulty in objective tests is knowing what answer the professor is seeking. Too often the questions are vague, misleading, nitpicking, or imprecise, and you are reduced to playing guessing games.

Try to use all the grammatical clues you can find by checking for plural or singular verbs, vowels, pronouns, and modifiers, as well as adverbs and adjectives. If you don't know the whole answer to a question, guess at it, if there is no penalty for wrong answers. You could receive partial credit or be lucky enough to guess right.

Completion Tests

On a completion test you simply fill in the answers to complete a statement. Again, use all the clues provided for you through grammar. If you don't know the answer, guess at it. The difficulty in the completion test is that you do not always know what the professor is seeking. Because of the limited information required in a completion test, it has become less popular, especially in college testing.

True-False Tests

True-false tests pose a special threat because they are so devious. Close attention must be paid to qualifying words, such as *first, second, last, always, never, generally, some-times, because, all, usually.* Remember that any section of a question or statement that is false makes the entire question or statement false. Teachers who compose true-false tests often seem to have demonic tendencies. The choice of information sought in the test is obscure. Play the game with old Beelzebub by being extra cautious.

Matching-Question Tests

These tests consist of two columns of statements and terms that must be matched. One column may have terms while the other one contains descriptions. Begin by pairing items of which you are certain. As you go along, you will find some of the answers become more clear simply by elimination. If you are uncertain of an answer, try to reason it through and take the time to read carefully. Look for key directional words or other grammatical clues. Again, beware of the qualifying words that shade meanings.

Multiple-Choice Tests

The multiple-choice tests are perhaps the most popular of all the objective tests because they can be used for mass testing and can be graded by machine. In addition, they can be used for every level of thinking ability, to estimate understanding, and to judge the student's ability to interpret and analyze.

The design of the multiple-choice test gives you the option of one of several choices of correct answers that are indicated by letters and numbers. At lower levels of education you simply choose the *one* correct answer. But at the college level, multiple-choice exams almost always require you to discern that there is *more than one* correct answer, and you must pinpoint the proper *combination* of correct answers. For example, choices may be (1) a; (2) a and d; (3) a, b, and c; (4) all of the above; (5) none of the above.

SUMMARY

If you are a well-organized person and follow the rules for studying effectively, know the techniques and skills involved in taking tests and examinations, and put these suggestions to work, you can be rewarded by receiving excellent grades. The result will be improved self-esteem, acceptance in the academic community, a good record for future reference, and greater joy in the adventures of learning.

29

Creative Problem Solving

Creativity is the encounter of the intensively conscious
human being with his world.

Rollo May

Creativity is not necessarily linked to invention, or artistic talent, or even intelligence as measured by the standard
IQ test. On any given day, you can and probably do fulfill
one of the dictionary definitions of creativity: "to bring into
being; to cause to exist." It is not strange or magical; it is
something you do all the time. Everyone is creative to some
degree.

You may wonder at this point whether or not it is worth
the effort to develop a plan for systematically evoking
creative thinking. "Why should I want to be more creative
when I am working hard trying to do my basic class assignments?" asked one returning student. Then, without
realizing it, he neatly demonstrated the essence of creativity as he unbuttoned the hood from his jacket and put a
bulky assortment of books inside it.

Perhaps even more important today than advances in
industry and the arts are the social institutions that make
our communities viable. Creative solutions are needed in

education, religion, the family, and government, ranging from the care of the aged to the use of energy, from the control of inflation to the financing of education. It is likely you are or will be working in similar areas.

A CREATIVE MIND SET

Do not think that unusual courses or stimulating professors must be part of the setting for creative endeavors. One professor's habitual absences without notice to the students led one of us to the library during that class hour. There the work of Carl Jung was discovered, which in turn led to the development of a special writing course that was later taught to university students. Luck and happenstance do play a part in creativity. Where you are at a particular place in time determines your direction. Although some people create their own luck, an offhand remark, a book read, or a scene viewed can be the catalyst of ideas.

Also, dispel the notion that everything of novelty or value has already been discovered. Stop and consider that all Western music is based on a twelve-note scale, all English literature on a twenty-six-letter alphabet, and all paintings represent a combination of three primary colors. If your product of recombination has value to you—as in the case of the hood becoming a carrying case for books— or to your culture, it is a worthwhile creation.

Never think you are too old to be creative. Like an account in a bank that has been drawing interest, older students have more living experience on which to draw. A woman who returned to school at age fifty-five to complete her degree in education recalls that her most creative effort was put into a six-week lesson plan she designed for her students. "All the experience I gained volunteering in school for my four children when they were small helped me. Ideas began to flow."

The nice thing about creativity is that it can be directed consciously; it is a learnable act. There are proven techniques, many of which are taught at special institutes such as the Creative Problem Solving Institute at the State

University of New York at Buffalo and Synectics Inc., of Cambridge, Massachusetts.

At Synectics, a private organization that has taught creative problem strategies to more than 10,000 clients since 1960, founder George Prince, of Arthur D. Little, says, "In the laboratory we learn to oscillate between playful, even outrageous thinking and being serious. Speculation and play make you ready for your problem. Later you can become more precise in the process of connecting things that have not been connected before. This approach applies to artistic problems, technical problems, personal problems, and business problems."

When we returned to school, we were fortunate to attend an innovative university. Students had great leeway in deciding on projects to aid their work. Consquently, when we wished to try our hand at fiction we asked to respond to some literature assignments with original stories. The stories weren't very good artistically, but the answers to the assignment were deeply embedded in them.

By convincing those in charge of your education to allow you more freedom to speculate in a less restrictive and less punitive climate, you may change yourself and the world around you. As a mature student, be confident and talk to your professor. Tell him one of the things you want to do is to become more creative and less locked into stereotypical learning patterns in the process of your learning. Ask, for example, if you can do an assignment in a way you see appropriate to this goal.

Earlier we said that critical thinking was one of the most important skills you will learn in college. To that we now add its complement—speculation and play.

MORE STRATEGIES

Some techniques designed to direct your creativity need no endorsement from teachers. The following is only a partial list and suggests a few we have found helpful in our own work. Any of these can be done by yourself or with a group you form.

Brainstorming

This is an uninhibited conference-type approach devised by Alex F. Osborn in 1938. The purpose of brainstorming is to produce the greatest possible number of ideas. The ground rules are:

1. Judgment must be withheld until all ideas are expressed.
2. Thinking off the top of the head is welcome.
3. Quantities of ideas are sought.
4. Combining and improving other group members' ideas is encouraged.

Don't stop too soon. The quality of ideas seems to improve as the brainstorming session progresses. One day-long session was devised by students in a child development course to formulate an opinion about a day care center on campus and its operation. Many of those suggestions were incorporated into the final plan.

Catalog Method

Find ideas in unrelated sources. Review newspapers, magazines, and catalogs, such as the index file in your own library, that will suggest ideas. Do not be afraid of borrowing ideas. Reslant them to make them uniquely yours.

Big Dream Technique

Imagine that your most appealing dream related to your school career, home, job, or personal life—or to mankind in general—can become a reality. Persistently study and think about every aspect and subject connected with that dream. Then drop some of the most fantastical points and make the dream come true.

In addition to the above strategies, seek out like minds in peer groups. Find them in professional societies, conventions, and workshops where an exchange of information and psychic energy will nourish you. Ask your professor to direct you to them, or check the *Directory of Associations* in your library.

If you continue to feel hopelessly uncreative, you could be blocking yourself with negative attitudes. Here are some attitudes you should try to avoid if you find that they apply to your behavior:

- Fear of making mistakes or appearing foolish.
- Grabbing the first idea that comes along because of a desire for security.
- Lack of drive or energy to carry problems through to a solution.
- Avoiding others who can help you because of mistrust or fear of associates and superiors.
- Inflexibility and biases that do not allow a new mental set or a compromise.
- Failure to investigate the obvious or what others may consider trivial or unimportant.

Creative problem solving requires openness to new experiences and a certain amount of risk taking. Fortunately, we are never too old to develop these qualities to fulfill our potential.

Meanwhile, keep in mind that the payoffs for participating in creative thinking are significant. While a college degree opens the job market door, creative thinking will advance you among those who prize the new and the valuable. If the thought of just passing grades and staying in school is not sufficiently meaningful, perhaps you will want to put your creative side into high gear.

TWO HEMISPHERES OF THE BRAIN

Our brain holds emotions, ideas, and memories. Its convoluted mass is the seat of our humanity. Art and science live here. The potential equivalent of 20 million volumes can be stored in every normal human brain. Even in sleep

our brains remain active, flashing with all kinds of complicated business. As astronomer and author Carl Sagan
notes, "Our passion for learning is the tool for our survi-
val."

Scientists have only recently begun studies to investigate
the different modes of expression of the brain's two hemispheres. Their impact on our future education could be
great; therefore, we think it is an important area for students to consider because it is seen as a vital link in the
way we learn. These studies are in fact changing the way
we think about thinking.

As far back as 1936, differences in the brain were noted.
Then, as now, most of the knowledge about hemisphere
specialization was based on studies done with brain-
damaged patients. In the 1960s, Dr. Joseph Bogen, a neuro-
surgeon in Los Angeles, severed the connection between
the two sides of the brain in his patients with severe
epilepsy. Tests performed later showed that the brain processed information and solved problems in two different
ways. It appeared each side had its own independent learning process and its own memory system. While the left side
controlled important functions such as speech and language skills, the right side of the brain controlled spatial
perception and body awareness and movement. (Because
the nerve fibers cross between the hemispheres, the left
side of the brain controls the motion of the right side of the
body and vice versa.)

Our educational system has always stressed the importance of left-brain function, which is analytical and
logical—the kind of thinking inherent in the fields of law,
medicine, and psychology. All of our cultural wisdom has
been passed along by left-hemisphere function. The functions of the right side of the brain, with its free-flowing
image production giving rise to the musician, artist, or
architect, have been thought to be of a lesser quality. "In
fact, until recently," says David Galin, a University of
California scientist in San Francisco, "the right hemisphere

of the brain was thought to be a stupid spare part for the left."

Despite the importance of the right brain and its capabilities for creativity, Western society's educational system has placed a premium on left-hemisphere functions, which are easier to test through the acquisition of number facts and reading skills. Because the right hemisphere is nonverbal, it is difficult, if not impossible, to describe the experiences of the imagery it produces. Psychologist Jerome Bruner, who has contributed much to our understanding of consciousness, says this of the right side of the brain: "It generates a grammar of its own, searching out connections, suggesting similarities, weaving ideas loosely in a trial web. . . . It is a way that grows happy hunches and 'lucky' guesses, that is stirred into connective activity by the poet and the necromancer looking sidewise rather than directly. . . . If he (man) is not fearful of these products of his own subjectivity, he will go so far as to tame the metaphors that have produced the hunches, tame them in the sense of shifting them from the left hand (right hemisphere to the right hand (left hemisphere) by rendering them into notions that can be tested."

It is possible that, through the conditioning of brain hemispheres, a whole new range of creative activity and psychic exploration may be awaiting us. The capacity to utilize both sides of the brain fully, in synchrony, may well result in significant achievements for future generations.

30

Looking Toward the Future

> We should be concerned about the future because we
> will have to spend the rest of our lives there.
>
> Charles F. Kettering

As we move through the '80s, increasing opportunities
for lifetime learners will continue to grow for all segments
of our society—the rich, the poor, the old, the young, and
middle-class America. By the year 2000, reports the
Carnegie Council of Policies Studies, one-fourth of all college students will be members of a minority.

With the diminished enrollment of the eighteen- to
twenty-two-year-old population on traditional campuses,
the lifelong learning explosion will be promoted for its
obvious virtues and to help finance a sagging educational
market. In addition to the educational establishment, the
role of the federal government in the university's policy
and governing systems will probably continue to grow,
with special consideration given to adults as effective educational consumers and the role of nontraditional education
in America.

As great as the challenge of developing new programs
and a new student body will be the challenge of distribut-

ing information regarding learning opportunities, career counseling, personal counseling, and financial aid. Colleges will move more of their faculty to on-site locations to teach courses and to advertise their wares; storefront posts, staffed with professionals to advise drop-ins about career and educational opportunities, may eventually be found in all major cities and towns. Specialized newsletters, magazines, and television and radio commercials will keep prospective students posted on current course offerings, letting them know where they can get what they need. Instead of using college catalogs and directories, students may rely on computer printouts that meet their specific needs, complete with mailing addresses, phone numbers, enrollment, test score averages, test and admission requirements, and costs.

Consumers of education will gain increasing access to computer information such as the Educational Resource Information Center (ERIC), which provides information on a wide variety of educational subjects through sixteen clearinghouses and three hundred libraries across the nation.

In short, as change takes place, Americans of all ages and backgrounds can look forward to an exciting, though possibly turbulent, decade in education.

If you can imagine what your future world should be like and how you might achieve it, you may want to open that door to college just a few short feet away from your grasp. Your foresight about your future depends on your ability to understand your needs. At the beginning of this book we asked you to write down those needs. We feel this concept of sorting out your priorities is so important that we ask you to repeat it, to write your own scenario.

You might begin this time by asking, "What would happen if. . . ." Imagine the various consequences of your action on finances, time, job, and care of children and spouse. Alert yourself to the potential problems that could accompany your preparations. At the same time view yourself with new skills and a new identity. Include in your scenario the use of experts—both academic and career counselors and teachers knowledgeable in your field of interest, and experts who can help you rectify any serious inadequacies in your basic skills. If the picture fits, then enter its framework.

For you this means an opportunity to explore the major fields of knowledge, to learn to help others as well as yourself to build a better life, to extend personal relationships, to learn new skills and upgrade old ones, and to finish what you started.

Whether or not you aspire to a career, the many doors to education stand ready to be unlocked with *your own personal key*. The odds are in your favor to find a better life on the other side. We certainly did, as we found an opportunity to be responsible for our own lives and achieve self-fulfillment.

Selective Bibliography

PART I

1. *Barron's Guide to the Two Year Colleges*, Vol. 1, College Descriptions, Sixth Edition, Woodbury, New York: Barron's Educational Series, 1978.

2. Blaze, Wayne, and Associates, *Guide to Alternative Colleges and Universities*, Boston, Massachusetts: Beacon Press, 1974.

3. Cass, James, and Birnaum, Max, *Comparative Guide to American Colleges*, Ninth Edition, New York: Harper and Row Publishers, 1979.

4. *CLEP—General and Subject Examinations*, Princeton, New Jersey: College Board Publishers, 1980.

5. *The College Blue Book, Narrative Description*, 17th Edition, New York: Macmillan Publishing Co., Inc., 1979.

6. Edelhart, Michael, *College Knowledge*, New York: Anchor Press, Doubleday, 1979.

7. "Freshman Wanted," *The Wall Street Journal*, Vol. LX, No. 128, 1980, p. 1.

8. Lawrence, Marcia, *How to Take the SAT,* New York, London, Ontario: New American Library, 1979.

9. Lovejoy, Clarence E., *Lovejoy's College Guide,* Fourteenth Edition, New York: Simon and Schuster, 1979.

10. Nyquist, Ewald B.; Arbolino, Jack; and Hawes, Gene R., *College Learning Anytime, Anywhere,* New York, London: Harcourt, Brace, Jovanovich, 1977.

11. Rogers, Carl R., *Freedom to Learn,* Columbus, Ohio: Charles E. Merrill, 1979.

12. Thomson, Frances C., *The New York Times Guide to Continuing Education in America,* College Entrance Examination Board, 1972.

13. Zucker, Fred, and Collier, Karen, *Peterson's Guide to College Admissions: How to Put the Odds on Your Side,* New York: Simon and Schuster, 1977.

PART II

1. *The College Blue Book,* 17th Edition, *Loans, Grants, Fellowships, and Scholarships,* New York: Macmillan Publishing Co., Inc., 1979.

2. Keeslar, Oreon, *Financial Aids for Higher Education,* '80--81 *Catalogue,* William C. Brown Co., Publishers.

3. Leider, Robert, *Your Own Financial Aid Factory, The Guide to Locating College Money,* Alexandria, Virginia: Octameron Associates, Inc., 1980.

4. "1980 Guide to Office of Education Programs," U.S. Department of Health, Education and Welfare (Washington, DC: U.S. Government Printing Office).

5. Porter, Sylvia, *New Money Book for the '80s,* Vol. 1, New York: Doubleday & Company, Inc., 1979.

6. "Meeting College Costs," Princeton, New Jersey: College Entrance Examination Board, 1979.

7. "Student Consumer's Guide, Six Federal Financial Aid Programs, 1980–81" (pamphlet), U.S. Department of Health, Education and Welfare (Washington, DC: U.S. Government Printing Office).

PART III

1. Barzun, Jacques, *The American University,* New York: Harper and Row, 1968.

2. Berman, Eleanor, *Re-entering, Successful Back to Work Strategies for Women Seeking a Fresh Start,* New York: Crown Publishers, Inc., 1980.

3. Glasser, William, *Positive Addiction,* 1st Edition, New York: Harper and Row, 1975.

4. Kennedy, Mopsy, S., "A for Affairs," *Glamour,* August 1980, p. 236.

5. Lamont, Lansing, *Campus Shock,* New York: E. P. Dutton, 1980.

6. Leefelt, Christine, and Callenbach, Ernest, *The Art of Friendship,* New York: Pantheon Books, 1979.

7. Mandell, Richard D., *The Professor Game,* Garden City, New York: Doubleday, 1977.

8. Modalfsky, Annie, *Welcome to the Real World,* New York: Doubleday, 1980.

9. O'Neill, Nena, and O'Neill, George, *Shifting Gears*, New York: M. Evans, 1974.

10. Rochelle, Larry, "Sex Roles on Campus: Does Professor Charles Really Get His Angel?", *Community College Frontiers*, Vol. 8, #4, Sangamon State University, Springfield, Illinois, Summer 1980.

11. Rogers, Carl R., *A Way of Being*, Boston, Massachusetts: Houghton Mifflin Company, 1980.

12. Voeks, Virginia, *On Becoming an Educated Person*, Philadelphia, London, Toronto: W. B. Saunders Co., 1979.

13. Waitley, Dr. Denis, *The Winner's Edge*, New York: Times Books, 1980.

14. Wilke, Arthur S., *The Hidden Professorate*, Westport, Connecticut: Greenwood Press, 1979.

PART IV

1. Daniels, Arlene Kaplan, "Women and Neglect: The Ambiguous Reception of Re-entry Women at a Private, Elite University," Northwestern University, Evanston, Illinois.

2. *Letter to Ellen W. Collidge* as quoted by "A Judicial Document on Student Discipline," U.S. District Court, Western District of Missouri, *en banc* 1968, quoted in Ratliff, Richard C., *Constitutional Rights of College Students: A Study in Case Law*, Metuchen, New Jersey: The Scarecrow Press, 1972, pp. 13–14.

3. Mangano, Joseph A., and Corrado, Thomas J., "Meeting Academic Success Needs of Re-entry Adults," Albany, New York: New York State Education Department: ERIC Documentation EDI 69967, 1978.

4. "Man of the House," *The Wall Street Journal,* 16 October 1980, p. 1.

5. Marchese, Theodore J., "Restructuring a College to Meet Postsecondary Educational Needs of Non-College-Age Women," Washington, DC: Health, Education and Welfare, ERIC Documentation EDI 62549, 1975.

6. Newman, Stephen A., and Kramer, Nancy, *Getting What You Deserve,* New York: Dolphin Books, Doubleday & Co., 1979.

7. Parrino, John J., *From Panic to Power: The Positive Use of Stress,* New York: John Wiley and Sons, 1976.

8. Selye, Hans, M.D., *The Stress of Life,* New York: McGraw-Hill Book Company, 1976.

PART V

1. Adler, Mortimer J., *How to Read a Book,* New York: Simon and Schuster, 1940.

2. Aghassi, Marjorie Ewing, *Getting Good Grades,* Englewood Cliffs, New Jersey: Prentice-Hall, 1980.

3. Altick, Richard, *The Scholar Adventurers,* New York: The Macmillan Co., 1966.

4. Baker, Sheridan, *The Practical Stylist,* Ninth Edition, New York: Thomas Crowell, 1966.

5. Barnet, Sylvan; Berman, Morton; and Burto, William, *An Introduction to Literature,* Fourth Edition, Boston: Little, Brown and Co., 1971.

6. Broschart, James R., *Lifelong Learning in the Nation's Third Century,* U.S. Department of Health, Education and Welfare (Washington, DC: U.S. Government Printing Office), 1977.

7. Bruner, Jerome S., *Beyond the Information Given*, New York: W. W. Norton, 1973.

8. Buzan, Tony, *Use Both Sides of Your Brain*, New York: E. P. Dutton, 1976.

9. Feder, Bernard, *The Complete Guide to Taking Tests*, Englewood Cliffs, New Jersey: Prentice-Hall, Inc., 1979.

10. Gagne, Robert M., *The Conditions of Learning*, Second Edition, New York: Holt, Rinehart and Winston, Inc., 1970.

11. Gowan, John Curtis, and Olson, Meredith, "The Society Which Maximizes Creativity," *The Journal of Creative Behavior*, Vol. 13 #3, Third Quarter.

12. Gross, Ronald, *The Lifelong Learner*, New York: Simon and Schuster, 1977.

13. Huxley, A., *The Art of Seeing*, Seattle: Montana Books, 1975.

14. Jaroslovsky, Rich, "Brain Hemisphere Seen as Vital Factor in Way We Learn," *The Wall Street Journal*, March 30, 1979, p. 1

15. "You and Creativity," *Kaiser Aluminum News*, Vol. 25 #3.

16. Kidd, J. R., *How Adults Learn*, New York: Association Press, 1978.

17. Koestler, Arthur, *The Act of Creation*, New York: The Macmillan Co., 1964.

18. Leedy, Paul, *Read with Speed and Efficiency*, New York: McGraw-Hill, 1963.

19. Maddox, Harry, *How to Study*, New York: Fawcett Premier, 1963.

20. May, Rollo, *The Courage to Create*, New York: W. W. Norton, 1975.

21. McCallum, Steve R., and Glynn, Shaw, "Hemispheric Specialization and Creative Behavior," *The Journal of Creative Behavior*, Vol. 13, #4, Fourth Quarter.

22. McCroskey, James C., *An Introduction to Rhetorical Communication*, Englewood Cliffs, New Jersey: Prentice-Hall, Inc., 1968.

23. McKim, Robert H., *Experiences in Visual Thinking*, Monterey, California: Brooks Cole, 1972.

24. Muter, Paul, "Very Rapid Forgetting,"*Memory and Cognition*, Vol. 8, #II, March 80, p. 174.

25. Norman, Donald A., *Memory and Attention*, New York: John Wiley and Sons, 1976.

26. Ornstein, Robert E., *The Psychology of Consciousness*, San Francisco: W. H. Freeman, 1972.

27. Pulaski, Mary Ann Spencer, *Understanding Piaget*, New York: Harper and Row, 1971.

28. Sabin, Louis, "10 Tricks to Improve Your Memory," *50+*, September 1979.

29. Sommer, Robert, *The Mind's Eye*, New York: Delacorte Press, 1978.

30. *35 Ways Colleges Are Serving Adult Learners*, Princeton, New Jersey: College Board Publications, 1979.

Index

DATE			

© THE BAKER & TAYLOR CO